Competitive Identity

COMPETITIVE IDENTITY

The New Brand Management for Nations, Cities and Regions

Simon Anholt

First published 2007 by
PALGRAVE MACMILLAN
Houndmills, Basingstoke, Hampshire RG21 6XS and
175 Fifth Avenue, New York, N.Y. 10010
Companies and representatives throughout the world

PALGRAVE MACMILLAN is the global academic imprint of the Palgrave Macmillan division of St. Martin's Press, LLC and of Palgrave Macmillan Ltd. Macmillan® is a registered trademark in the United States, United Kingdom and other countries. Palgrave is a registered trademark in the European Union and other countries.

ISBN-13: 978-0-230-50028-0
ISBN-10: 0-230-50028-5

This book is printed on paper suitable for recycling and made from fully managed and sustained forest sources. Logging, pulping and manufacturing processes are expected to conform to the environmental regulations of the country of origin.

A catalogue record for this book is available from the British Library.

A catalog record for this book is available from the Library of Congress.

Library Of Congress Catalogue Card Number - 2006050177

10   9   8   7   6   5   4   3
16   15   14   13   12   11   10   09   08   07

Printed and bound in Great Britain by
Cromwell Press, Trowbridge, Wilts

CONTENTS

LIST OF FIGURES

List of Tables

Introduction

I first began to write about an idea I called *nation branding* in 1996. My original observation was a simple one: that the reputations of countries are rather like the brand images of companies and products, and equally important.

The idea of brand management is still an important part of my work, but I now call the approach *Competitive Identity*, because it has more to do with national identity and the politics and economics of competitiveness than with branding as it is usually understood.

Ten years on seems like a good moment to pause and take stock of where this thinking has led, and how the field has developed: because it is a field today, with its commercial and academic communities, consulting firms, publications, conferences, research, and a rising number of full-time professionals in national, city and regional administrations.

This book is an attempt to collect together some of the practical experience, theories, research and case notes I have gathered during this exciting decade of intense activity and learning, and to present the current state of my arguments for the role of brand management in national policy, strategy and development.

It isn't my intention to give a detailed "recipe" for creating Competitive Identity, because there is no standard formula: the process must always be a collaborative one, and of course every place has its own aims, circumstances, resources and competences. So I have limited myself to describing the theory of Competitive Identity, and a sketch of the main drivers, challenges and opportunities in the field, interspersed with some case notes.

One of the reasons why I continue to find this subject appealing is because it's such a big intellectual, moral and philosophical challenge: these are genuinely difficult concepts to grasp, to employ and to communicate. For a long time I was puzzled by this, as I somehow didn't expect the subject to be so demanding: branding is, after all, only a quasi-science related to shopping. I now realize that although the usual context of brand theory may be buying and selling and promoting consumer goods, this is a thin layer that covers some of the hardest philosophical questions one can tackle: the nature of perception and reality, the relationship between objects and their representation, the phenomena of mass psychology, the mysteries of national identity, leadership, culture and social cohesion, and much more besides.

The idea that I call Competitive Identity is already much more than an academic curiosity at the fringes of marketing: it is now the intense focus of many, if not most, governments. Ten years ago, my conversations on the subject were largely theoretical, and mainly with marketing academics. Now the talk is far more urgent and practical, and it is with ministers, ambassadors, city mayors and regional administrations, international organizations and donor agencies, heads of government and heads of state.

Today, every place on earth wants to do something to manage its international reputation; yet we are still very far from a widespread understanding of what this means in practice, and just how far commercial approaches can be effectively and responsibly applied to government, society and economic development. Many governments, most consultants and even some scholars persist in a naïve and superficial interpretation of "nation branding" that is nothing more than standard product promotion, public relations and corporate identity, where the product just happens to be a country rather than a bank or a running shoe.

So at this point, Competitive Identity or nation branding could go two ways. If the naïve model becomes dominant, and causes a sufficient number of countries and cities and donors to waste sufficient amounts of money on futile propaganda, it will fail to gain any credibility with policy makers, and will simply go out of fashion.

If, on the other hand, the growing community of thinkers and practitioners in the field does manage to raise the discussion to the level of intellect, responsibility, expertise and maturity that it needs and deserves, it could be a very different story. Just as brand management has proved to be one of the most potent instruments for devising strategy and creating wealth in the commercial sector, so its application to the development and competitiveness of states, regions and cities could have enormous and far-reaching impacts in the years to come.

It is my hope that this book can play a part in ensuring that in another ten years' time, the tale I will have to tell will be closer to the latter than the former.

London   SIMON ANHOLT

CHAPTER 1

What is Competitive Identity?

Today, the world is one market. The rapid advance of globalization means that every country, every city and every region must compete with every other for its share of the world's consumers, tourists, investors, students, entrepreneurs, international sporting and cultural events, and for the attention and respect of the international media, of other governments, and the people of other countries.

In such a busy and crowded marketplace, most of those people and organizations don't have time to learn about what other places are really like. We all navigate through the complexity of the modern world armed with a few simple clichés, and they form the background of our opinions, even if we aren't fully aware of this and don't always admit it to ourselves: Paris is about style, Japan about technology, Switzerland about wealth and precision, Rio de Janeiro about carnival and football, Tuscany about the good life, and most African nations about poverty, corruption, war, famine and disease. Most of us are much too busy worrying about ourselves and our own countries to spend too long trying to form complete, balanced and informed views about six billion other people and nearly 200 other countries. We make do with summaries for the vast majority of people and places – the ones we will probably never know or visit – and only start to expand and refine these impressions when for some reason we acquire a particular interest in them.

When you haven't got time to read a book, you judge it by its cover.

These clichés and stereotypes – whether they are positive or negative, true or untrue – fundamentally affect our behaviour towards other places and their people and products. It may seem unfair, but there's nothing anybody can do to change this. It's very hard for a country to persuade people in other parts of the world to go beyond these simple images and start to understand the rich complexity that lies behind them.

Some quite progressive countries don't get nearly as much attention, visitors, business or investment as they need because their reputation is weak or negative, while others are still trading on a good image that they acquired decades or even centuries ago, and today do relatively little to deserve.

The same is true of cities and regions: all the places with good, powerful and positive reputations find that almost everything they undertake on the international stage is easier; and the places with poor reputations find that almost everything is difficult, and some things seem virtually impossible.

So all responsible governments, on behalf of their people, their institutions and their companies, need to discover what the world's perception of their country is, and to develop a strategy for managing it. It is a key part of their job to try to build a reputation that is fair, true, powerful, attractive, genuinely useful to their economic, political and social aims, and which honestly reflects the spirit, the genius and the will of the people. This huge task has become one of the primary skills of government in the twenty-first century.

Today, most countries promote their products and services and steer their reputation as best they can, but they seldom do it in a coordinated way:

- the tourist board promotes the country to holidaymakers and business travellers
- the investment promotion agency promotes the country to foreign companies and investors
- the cultural institute builds cultural relations with other countries and promotes the country's cultural and educational products and services
- the country's exporters promote their products and services abroad
- the Ministry of Foreign Affairs presents its policies to overseas publics in the best possible light, and sometimes attempts to manage the national reputation as a whole.

In most countries, there are many other bodies, agencies, ministries, special interest groups, non-governmental organizations (NGOs) and companies all promoting their version of the country too.

Since most of these bodies, official and unofficial, national and regional, political and commercial, are usually working in isolation, they send out conflicting and even contradictory messages about the country. As a result, no consistent picture of the country emerges, and its overall reputation stands still or moves backwards.

Far more can be achieved if the work of these stakeholders is coordinated, of consistently high quality, and harmonized to an overall national strategy that sets clear goals for the country's economy, its society and its political and cultural relations with other countries. This is a role that none of the conventional disciplines of public diplomacy or sectoral promotion is able to perform alone.

However, the task of promotion, positioning and reputation management on a global scale is a familiar one in the world of commerce: corporations have been facing it for more than a century, and this is how the techniques of brand management have emerged.

Clearly there are more differences than similarities between countries and companies, but some of the theories and techniques of brand management can, if intelligently and responsibly applied, become powerful competitive tools and agents for change both within the country and beyond.

Competitive Identity (or CI) is the term I use to describe the synthesis of brand management with public diplomacy and with trade, investment, tourism and export promotion. CI is a new model for enhanced national competitiveness in a global world, and one that is already beginning to pay dividends for a number of countries, cities and regions, both rich and poor.

Why branding has a bad brand

The presence of brand management at the heart of this approach to national competitiveness does present a problem. There's a lot of mistrust about brands and branding these days, and this isn't helped by the fact that nobody seems to agree on what the words really mean.

Branding is a topic that's constantly in the media, and as consumers we are in contact with brands every day, so naturally we all have our own idea of what brands and branding are all about. Most of us think that "branding" is roughly synonymous with advertising, graphic design, promotion, public relations (PR) or even propaganda. Marketers and advertisers and other people who work professionally with brands use different and more technical definitions of the words, and their definitions can vary from one industry to another.

Whenever branding is spoken about in the context of countries, regions or cities – as it is with increasing frequency today – people tend to assume that these promotional techniques are simply being used to "sell" the country; and not surprisingly, they don't like the sound of that. More than one journalist has compared the branding of places to the branding of cattle: applying an attractive logo, a catchy slogan, and marketing the place as if it were nothing more than a product in the global supermarket.

Vocabulary is also important when making the case for national brand management and public diplomacy: there is definitely something inflammatory about the language of marketing. Marketers have long been in the habit of talking cavalierly about the techniques of persuasion, coldly classifying people into consumer types, "controlling the drivers of behaviour", and so on. It's a vocabulary which, if you're not used to it, sounds cynical, arrogant, even sinister, and politicians would do well not to imitate it too closely, no matter how modern they may think it makes them sound.

So there is a danger when discussing brands, and especially new ideas such as the application of brand theory to countries, that the discussion turns into what psychologists call *cognitive dissonance*: everybody is talking at cross-purposes, pursuing an almost private conversation based on their own understanding of the word, and there is little communication.

The concept of Competitive Identity uses the idea of brands and branding in a specific way that is rather different from the way that ordinary consumers use it, and in some cases different from the ways that professional marketing people do. For this reason, it is a good idea to start off with some definitions.

What is a brand?

First, we need to make a clear distinction between *brands* and *branding*:

- a *brand* is a product or service or organization, considered in combination with its name, its identity and its reputation
- *branding* is the process of designing, planning and communicating the name and the identity, in order to build or manage the reputation.

I will explain later why the distinction is important when we're dealing with nations, but a fundamental argument in this book is that although nations and regions and cities do *have* brand images, they can't usually *be* branded: at least not in the way that products, services or companies can.

It's also important to distinguish between four different aspects of the brand itself: brand *identity,* brand *image,* brand *purpose* and brand *equity*.

The *brand identity* is the core concept of the product, clearly and distinctively expressed. For commercial products and services, it is what we see in front of us as consumers: a logo, a slogan, packaging, the design of the product itself. This aspect of brand has some parallels with the idea of national identity, but the comparison is a tricky one. The techniques of brand communication, such as graphic design, for example, don't have much relevance for countries, since countries aren't single products or organizations that can be "branded" in this sense.

The *brand image* is the perception of the brand that exists in the mind of the consumer or audience – it's virtually the same thing as reputation – and it may or may not match the brand identity. It includes a range of associations, memories, expectations and other feelings that are bound up with the product, the service, or the company. These feelings are important drivers of people's behaviour, so brand image is a critical concept when we're talking about nations, cities and regions.

Brand image is the context in which messages are received: it's not the message itself. This point is difficult to explain in abstract terms, so I will give a hypothetical example: imagine there are two airlines that both decide to install double beds in their business class cabins, so couples can sleep together on longer flights. One of the airlines, Aeroflot, has a weak brand; the other, Virgin Atlantic, has a strong brand. The announcement about double beds from Aeroflot would probably be received with distaste by press and public alike; but precisely the same message from Virgin would be – and indeed was – received with enthusiastic approval. The message is identical, but the market response is opposite: and that is the effect of brand image.

This is the reason why it is often said that the owner of the trademark isn't the owner of the brand. The brand image doesn't reside in the company's offices or factories, but in the mind of the consumer: in other words, in a remote location. And, useful though it would be for companies to penetrate the mind of the consumer and manipulate that brand, of course they can't. So the remote location is also a secure location. And finally, there is no single consumer with one single mind: the brand image is dispersed across millions upon millions of consumers, each one with a different perspective of the brand. So the brand image exists in a remote, secure, distributed location, which makes talk about "building" and "managing" the brand image sound very much like wishful thinking: companies can tinker with the brand identity as much as they like, but whether this affects the brand image is another matter.

Another important concept is what I call *brand purpose*, an idea that is similar to corporate culture; it can be considered as the internal equivalent of brand image. Corporations, and especially the ones with powerful brands, often talk about this internal aspect of brand as "the spirit of the organization", "living the brand", "shared values" or "common purpose".

The idea is that an external promise to the marketplace has little meaning if it isn't shared by the workforce and other stakeholders, and if it isn't lived out in the internal structures, processes and culture of the organization. This is true of all groups of people, whether it's a company, a club, a sports team or a whole country: if most people accept the same values and share the same goals, the group is far more likely to achieve its objectives. And since the service element of companies today is a more and more important part of their competitive edge – most physical products being virtually identical – it makes sense that a strong internal culture, strongly wedded to the external promise of the organization, is likely to build a powerful reputation. This aspect of branding is also important when we're talking about countries, cities or regions.

Finally, the concept of *brand equity*. This phrase sums up the idea that if a company, product or service acquires a positive, powerful and solid reputation, this becomes an asset of enormous value: probably more valuable, in fact, than all the tangible assets of the organization itself, because it represents the company's ability to continue to trade at a healthy margin for as long as its brand image stays intact. Brand equity also represents the "permission" given by the company's loyal consumer base for it to continue producing and developing its product range, innovating, communicating and selling to them. This goodwill, if measured in dollar terms, is often worth many times more than the balance sheet of the company, which is why companies with powerful brands often change hands at an enormous premium: one isn't simply acquiring real estate, stock and machinery, but a trusting relationship with a segment of the marketplace. Without its brand equity, for example, the market capitalization of a company such as Xerox would be a mere $481 million rather than $6.5 billion.[1]

A good brand name is a valuable thing for producers to have: it's the thing that gets their product noticed, and stops it vanishing among the thousands of competing, nearly identical products. It means that when they launch a new product under the same name, people give it a try. It means that people stay loyal to their products, even if, from time to time, they aren't the best, the newest or the easiest to use. The maker's good name reassures us that time, money and expertise have been invested in making it as good as possible; it's also a promise that if something goes wrong in a year's time, they'll still be around to put it right.

The brand name acts as our short cut to an informed buying decision. The more often we are proved right about our choice, and the more often the product or service lives up to the good name of the company that makes it, the more valuable that name becomes in our eyes.

Brand is undoubtedly a dangerous word, charged with many negative and emotive associations, but the concept of brand is a powerful one, and is uniquely important to the management of countries, cities and regions because it captures so well the idea that places need to understand and manage their internal identity and their external reputation.

Brand management uniquely embraces these important ideas of *core meaning* (brand identity), *reputation* (brand image), the *asset value of reputation* (brand equity), and the *power of shared goals* (brand purpose), and this is why it is a valuable source of inspiration for governments. It's unfortunate that most people's primary association with the word is the packaging and promotion of consumer goods, as it's the association that is least relevant to the notion of Competitive Identity, and the most distracting one: but there is simply no other word or concept that effectively links these four ideas into a single, coherent system.

Brand management and the nation

Every inhabited place on earth has a reputation, just as products and companies have brand images. The brand images of products and companies may be deliberately created through advertising and marketing, while the reputations of places tend to come about in a more complex and more random way, but the comparison is still a useful one, because in both cases the image has a profound impact on the fortunes of its "owner", and people's perceptions may have greater consequences than reality.

The reputation of a place may be rich and complex, or simple; it may be mainly negative or mainly positive. For most places, it's a constantly shifting mixture of the two.

The place may be internationally famous, such as the United States or Rio de Janeiro, which mean something for most of the world's population. It may be famous in one part of the world but unfamiliar elsewhere, such as the English Channel Isles or the Crimean Riviera. Or it may be completely unknown to everyone but its closest neighbours, such as Fruitful Vale in Jamaica, or Novolokti (a village in the Siberian region of Tyumen, in case you were wondering).

1 The place may mean much the same things to most people who are aware of it. This means it has a strong reputation.
2 If the place means very little to most people who are aware of it, or widely different things depending on who you ask, it has a weak reputation.
3 If it is known by a lot of people, it is a famous place.

Of course strong and famous don't necessarily mean positive: North Korea, Afghanistan and Iraq, for example, all have strong and famous reputations that are currently not positive.

The country's reputation powerfully affects the way people inside and outside the place think about it, the way they behave towards it, and the way they respond to everything that's made or done there. Ask yourself the following questions:

1 If you had a choice between two DVD players from unknown makers with identical features, would you expect to pay more for the Japanese brand or the Chinese brand?
2 If you had two equally qualified candidates for a senior management role, would you be more likely to pick the Turk or the Swede?
3 If the Mongolian State Circus and the Nigerian State Circus were in town, which one would you expect to be the better show?

4 Would you rather have your capital city twinned with Sydney or Sarajevo?

5 Does a holiday on the Albanian Riviera sound more or less luxurious than one on the French Riviera?

6 Would you build a technology factory just outside Zurich or just outside Kampala?

For each of these questions, there might be very good reasons for picking either option, but most people have a clear idea which they would pick, even when they don't know very much about either country.

The reputation of a country has a direct and measurable impact on just about every aspect of its engagement with other countries, and plays a critical role in its economic, social, political and cultural progress. Whether we're thinking about going somewhere on holiday, buying a product that's made in a certain country, applying for a job overseas, moving to a new town, donating money to a war-torn or famine-struck region, or choosing between films or plays or CDs made by artists in different countries, we rely on our perception of those places to make the decision-making process a bit easier, a bit faster, a bit more efficient.

Just like commercial brands, some of the glamour of that nation brand also reflects back on us for choosing it. It makes you feel stylish when you become the owner of something by Alessi or Gucci, and you get a similar feeling when you go to the Amalfi coast for your holiday, cook *penne all'arrabbiata*, take Italian lessons, listen to Pavarotti or name your children Lucia and Stefano.

Country of origin effect

Some countries – and Italy is a good example of this – add appeal to their exports in a way that seems completely effortless. Even very good products from other places, such as Guatemala or Belgium or Lithuania, somehow don't work the same magic.

Marketing academics call this the *country of origin effect*, and people have known for centuries that a "Made In ..." label is just as powerful and just as valuable as a "Made By ..." label. German engineering, French chic, Japanese miniaturization, Italian flair, Swedish design, British class, Swiss precision: these are brand values that rub off onto the products that come from those countries, and they count for a lot.

Country of origin effect is part of the reason why, in the early 1990s, Americans bought lots of Toyota Corollas (which were quite expensive) and not very many Geo Prizms (which were quite cheap), even though they were exactly the same car, made in the same factory. American consumers believed that Japanese cars offered greater value than American cars, so they bought the Toyota.

Consumers prefer to make informed buying decisions but they are short of time (and in the end, short of patience too: after all, even in the profoundly consumerist societies of Western Europe, Asia-Pacific or North America, people still don't want to spend *too* long worrying about products), and the country of origin of a product, just like a brand name, is believed to be a short cut to an informed buying decision. If the information is too complex, we will simply discard any part of it that we feel is of secondary importance, and revert to a simple belief: that's why most people, for example, still think of Range Rover, Aston Martin, Rolls-Royce, Bentley, Mini and Jaguar as being British cars, even though it is well known that they are all now owned by German or American companies.

In reality, that reassurance of value or quality we get from a "made in" label is only symbolic. Governments can't impose the same quality standards throughout their entire manufacturing sector, even in very rich (or totalitarian) countries. But faith is often more potent than logic, and perception often stronger than reality: that's just the way people are.

Country of origin effect is only one part of the picture, however, and countries depend on their reputations in many other ways. A country's good name doesn't just help consumers make millions of everyday purchasing choices, it affects much bigger decisions too: companies deciding where to build their factories, set up their overseas operations, market their products or outsource their industrial processes and customer service centres; governments deciding where to spend their foreign aid budgets; international sporting bodies, entertainment, talent or beauty contests deciding which country or city will host their next event; opera and theatre companies deciding where to tour; film studios deciding where to go on location; even governments picking their allies in times of international conflict.

This is because the organizations that make these big decisions are staffed by people who are still people. They are still consumers in their spare time, they still think like consumers and, even if they're usually anxious to deny it, their choices are affected partly by their expert knowledge and partly by their perceptions and prejudices. Even though these professional decision-makers go through exhaustive comparison and analysis of candidate countries, they still need ways to help make their initial shortlist, and ways to eliminate the identical contenders. In some cases, a bribe will do the trick, but the reputations of countries are equally good at "unsticking" these difficult decisions. In their hearts, the decision makers *know* which candidate they hope will win through.

Moreover, they also realize that their decision has to be the right one for an end user. Using facts alone to pick the host country for an international sporting event, for example, is fine up to a point, but in the end it has to be a location that the television audience finds exciting and appealing; athletes and spectators have to feel happy about travelling and staying there, and their perceptions or prejudices about the place can carry just as much weight as practical considerations such as cost, transport links and facilities.

The same applies when multinational companies are deciding where to build their overseas offices or factories: the management may choose a country on the basis of its infrastructure, climate, location, security, transport links, quality and location of supplier firms, business-friendly government, skilled workforce, tax breaks and incentive packages, but it's still the wrong decision if the managers who actually have to relocate there don't fancy the sound of that particular country. And even if they can be persuaded, can their families?

Perhaps it's not so surprising that such a big part is played by "mere image" or "mere reputation" in these decisions: as the economist Maurice Allais showed in 1953,[2] the more important and consequential a decision becomes, the more people are likely to rely on their feelings and intuition rather than logic to make the decision. There comes a point when decisions are just too critical for us to rely on our brains, and so we refer to our hearts. As the American banker J.P. Morgan wisely said: "A man always buys something for two reasons: a good reason, and the *real* reason."

Even people can suffer from country of origin effect, as is suggested by my earlier question about the nationality of candidates for a senior management role. People in the United Kingdom are now familiar with the idea of plumbers being Polish, which may be a good thing for Polish plumbers, but it could make life in the UK rather difficult for Polish pilots, chefs and surgeons.

It's no exaggeration to say that the reputation of a country has a profound impact on its social, cultural, economic and political destiny, but there's nothing very surprising or controversial about this. We are simply creatures who can only experience the world through our perceptions of it. The distinction between "perception" and "reality" is not a sharply-drawn line at all when you start to think about it, but a rather hazy philosophical notion.

Public diplomacy

Of the various ways in which countries and their governments represent themselves to the rest of the world, the area that has most in common with the brand management of companies is public diplomacy. It is public diplomacy, twinned with brand management, that underpins the idea of Competitive Identity.

The term "public diplomacy" was first used by the United States Information Agency in the early 1960s in an attempt to communicate what is meant when a modern state manages its reputation abroad.[3] The full definition of the term at the time was:

> the influence of public attitudes on the formation and execution of foreign policies. It encompasses dimensions of international relations beyond traditional diplomacy; the cultivation by governments of public opinion in other countries; the interaction of private groups and interests in one country with those of another; the reporting of foreign affairs and its impact on policy; communication between those whose job is communication, as between diplomats and foreign correspondents; and the processes of inter-cultural communications.

Jan Melissen of the Dutch foreign policy think-tank, Clingendael, uses the famous 1945 photograph of Roosevelt, Stalin and Churchill at the Yalta conference to illustrate how diplomacy has changed since the

Second World War, and how the concept of public diplomacy has emerged. All three leaders travelled, slowly and privately, by steamer to Yalta, where they sorted out the reconstruction of Europe and the new world order. Having done this, they sailed slowly back to their respective countries, after which the public was duly informed of their decisions. Melissen contrasts this staid and exclusive affair with twenty-first-century summits such as Geneva, Genoa and Seattle, which dominate the world's television screens for days on end, and where you can't move for journalists and protesters. Instant communications and widespread democracy are squeezing out old-fashioned private diplomacy: like it or not, international relations now take place in real time, before a global audience.

Modern public diplomacy often embraces much more than just the communications of government policies, and in some cases is virtually synonymous with Competitive Identity: for example, the US State Department and the UK Foreign and Commonwealth Office both use the term to describe the process by which they attempt to manage the entire national reputation.

These days, there is more collaboration and integration between embassies, cultural bodies and trade and tourist offices: modern diplomats see promoting trade, tourism, investment and culture as an important part of their job. But countries generally get the biggest improvement in their overall reputation when all the main sectors of the country are aligned to a common strategy. The Ministry of Foreign Affairs may or may not be the right body to lead this process in every case but, whatever the administrative structure, it's clear that all the major stakeholders of the country's image need to be fully represented on it; and this full representation is, as I will explain later, one of the basic principles for building Competitive Identity.

If the purpose of public diplomacy is simply to promote government policies, it is likely to be superfluous or futile, depending on the good name of the country or its government at that particular time: if the country is in favour, then unless the policy is patently wrong-headed, it is likely to be well received and simply needs to be communicated. Little art or skill are required to do this. If, on the other hand, the country suffers from a poor or weak reputation, then almost no amount of promotional skill or expenditure can cause the policy to be received with enthusiasm, and it will either be ignored or taken as further proof of whatever evil is currently ascribed to the country. This is why I earlier defined brand image as the *context in which messages are received*, not the messages themselves.

Wise people have always understood that people's perceptions of the messenger can be more important than the message. The English novelist Anthony Trollope makes exactly the same point in his 1881 novel, *Dr Wortle's School*:

> So much in this world depends on character that attention has to be paid to bad character even when it is not deserved. In dealing with men and women, we have to consider what they believe, as well as what we believe ourselves. The utility of a sermon depends much on the idea that the audience has of the piety of the man who preaches it. Though the words of God should never have come with greater power from the mouth of man, they will come in vain if they be uttered by one who is known as a breaker of the Commandments; they will come in vain from the mouth of one who is even suspected to be so.

For this reason, public diplomacy is virtually useless unless it has some power to affect the background reputation of the country whose policies it attempts to represent; and since that background reputation can only be altered by policies, not by communications, the critical success factor for public diplomacy is whether its connection to policy making is one-way or two-way. If there is a two-way mechanism that allows the public diplomacy function to pass back recommendations for policy making, and these recommendations are taken seriously and properly valued by government as critical "market feedback", then public diplomacy has a chance of enhancing the good name of the country, thus ensuring that future policy decisions are received in a more favourable light. It's a virtuous circle, because of course under these circumstances the policies need far less "selling".

Simply ensuring that the public diplomacy function has an influence over government policies, however, can have only a limited impact on the background reputation of countries. It is only when public diplomacy is carried out in coordination with the full complement of national stakeholders as well as the main policy makers, and all are linked through effective brand management to a single, long-term national strategy, that the country has a real chance of affecting its image and making it into a competitive asset rather than an impediment or a liability.

Marketing and governance

The leaders of countries have been trying to find ways of capturing the force of public opinion since the beginning of time, both domestically and internationally, so in that sense there is nothing very new about the idea of Competitive Identity, even if the expression is a new one in this context. Ever since there have been leaders, there has been an awareness of the power of a strong reputation as an aid to achieving one's political, social, economic and cultural aims.

There is nothing very new either about the idea of using techniques from the commercial sector to promote the good name of countries and cities and their governments: it has been the habit of American administrations for more than a century to call in the advertising men, the PR gurus, the speechwriters and the spin doctors whenever there's a job of mass persuasion to be done. And it's not just America: the reputations of many places have been deliberately built and managed by their leaders over the centuries, and those leaders have often borrowed expertise from others to augment their political skills: from poets, orators, philosophers, movie-makers, artists and writers.

Only recently, though, has the discipline of marketing been judged to have something useful to contribute to policy making, economic or social development and international relations: in other words, not just to promotion, but to strategy. Marketing is coming of age in many ways, and as the developed world has become organized more and more along commercial lines, it has become clear that a science which shows you how to persuade large numbers of people to change their minds about things has all kinds of interesting applications.

So it's no longer just businesses that recognize the usefulness of marketing: political parties, governments, charities, good causes, state bodies and NGOs are turning to marketing as they begin to understand that profound truth that marketers always knew: being in possession of the truth is not enough: the truth has to be *sold*.

However, the elevation of commercial marketing disciplines to the dizzying heights of national strategy does create tensions. At the heart of the issue is the old question of whether marketing is merely about selling things, or something altogether more strategic. It doesn't help that so many politicians – just like most ordinary consumers – think that building a brand is simply a matter of designing a new logo for their country and a slogan to go underneath it.

Building Competitive Identity is a much bigger and more complex task than this, as this book will attempt to show. There is no area of commercial marketing that approaches the depth and breadth of a true CI strategy, with its agenda of imposing creativity, consistency, truthfulness and effectiveness onto a wide range of difficult fields including the development and promotion of national and regional tourism, inward investment, recruitment and trade; the branding of exports; international relations and foreign policy; social and cultural policy; urban and environmental planning; economic development; membership of supranational bodies; diasporas; sport; media management; and much else besides.

In fact, I would claim that the first and most important component of any national CI strategy is creating a spirit of benign nationalism amongst the populace, notwithstanding its cultural, social, ethnic, linguistic, economic, political, territorial and historical divisions. This is a very long way from the kind of challenge that product marketers usually have to face on a Monday morning; and yet at the same time, it is a challenge that would remind most of them strongly of their own need to make stakeholders in the corporation "live the brand".

It does seem an odd place for brand management, a humble commercial service, to find itself: almost, in a sense, teaching governments how to govern more effectively. But the fact is that governments now find themselves competing in ways that they are scarcely prepared to deal with, and inhabiting a world of global competition and mobile consumers where few of their traditional approaches really work. This is a world that companies know well, and where they have learned how to survive and prosper.

For this and many other reasons, I have become convinced that the disciplines of marketing and branding can, if wisely and responsibly adapted, bring value to pretty much any area of human endeavour, including national government and international relations.

I don't know of any other disciplines which – at their best – so fully explain and allow for the management of human enterprise: this unique marriage of empirical observation with visionary strategy. Marketing and branding combine scientific clarity of thought and rigorous observation of human psychology, culture and society with the more elusive factor of creativity. They combine advanced knowledge management (as is found in the way the better brands are handled in all their complex variants) with sensitive intercultural management (as is found in the way the better brands are communicated worldwide). They form a clear set of universally-applicable rules for building successful endeavours. They bring commerce and culture together as a potent force for creating prosperity. They can harness the power of language and images to bring about widespread social change (think of the hundreds of social campaigns around the world that have successfully taught people over the decades to wear safety belts in cars, to smoke less, to immunize their children, to pick up litter, to give to charity, to donate organs).

Good marketing and brand management have the humanity and wisdom to know that there is a difference between what makes sense on paper and how people actually behave: they have the intelligence of academia combined with the worldliness of practice.

Marketing and branding, in short, are among the notable achievements of the developed world, even if they have usually been used for more trivial ends, only increasing wealth where more wealth is least needed. But that's another discussion that really needs a whole book to explore,[4] although I'll touch on it in Chapter 6.

Competitive Identity is certainly one of the ways in which brand management can begin to realize its broader potential, and provides an opportunity to demonstrate that the discipline has something to contribute above and beyond that tired old litany of "increasing shareholder value".

Since the most commonly held understanding of branding outside sophisticated marketing departments tends to be "logos and slogans", it is hardly surprising that serious policy makers have in the past been reluctant to accept that this approach can bring anything of truly central importance to their work. Yet there is undoubtedly a growing acceptance in public affairs that a familiarity with the techniques of commercial marketing is increasingly relevant, and this may be something to do with the fact that the newer generations of politicians and civil servants now in their forties and fifties were raised in the age of the brand, and accept the importance of brand image and brand management as a matter of course.

That ministries of foreign affairs and their foreign services must practise something called public diplomacy – a discipline closely related to public relations – is now a commonplace; likewise the fact that public affairs has become an international affair, and that investment promotion and tourist promotion must be as sophisticated as the most sophisticated commercial marketing, since both are competing for consumer mindshare in the same space.

For a long time, however, the debate never seemed to go beyond the not very challenging truism that some lessons from the private sector can bring benefits to the ways in which countries and cities are marketed: a bit of public relations or media training can sharpen up diplomacy in the "media age"; a knowledge of Internet marketing and online media planning can make tourist boards more competitive; some attractive design can help investment promotion agencies in their work; and so forth.

If the usefulness of modern commercial practice to statecraft really did amount to this and nothing more, it would be difficult to justify the existence of this book. No, the reason why the convergence of advanced brand theory and statecraft is important is because brand management is a vital component of a new model for how places should be run in the future: it is the glue that binds together a range of different tools for national promotion and reputation management; tools that until now have only produced a fraction of their potential effect because they have been operating in a fragmented and inefficient way. Governments are just beginning to realize this, and to understand the competitive advantage that a nationally coordinated identity strategy can unlock.

The objection that the commercial model is associated with profits rather than people does not stand up to scrutiny. Brand management, when properly understood, is primarily about people, purpose and reputation, and only secondarily about money, although there is little question that organizations which are clear about their brand values and brand strategies ultimately stand a better chance of sustainable profitability than those which are not.

When I first began to write about "nation as brand", my observations were mainly focused on the country of origin effect. One of my first articles on the subject, "Nation Brands of the Twenty-First Century", argued that the countries in which certain products were manufactured (or were believed by consumers to be manufactured) functioned like brands in their own right. In the ten years since then, the arguments, the academic study around them, and the practitioner field itself have developed beyond recognition. Governments are beginning to wake up to the fact that cities, countries and regions all need a new way of looking at identity, strategy, development, competitiveness and purpose if they are to survive and prosper in a very new world order.

As Victor Hugo said, "There is one thing stronger than all the armies in the world, and that is an idea whose time has come" (*Histoire d'un Crime*: 1877).

Why the age of Competitive Identity has come

Big changes in the social and political fabric of modern society make the more "public-oriented" approach of Competitive Identity a necessity. This is not a question of governments "playing to the gallery" or a strategy for legitimizing state propaganda, just a growing acknowledgment of the influence of global public opinion and market forces on international affairs.

Below are listed a few of the conditions that now make a brand-oriented approach to competitiveness not just desirable but necessary.

1 The spread of democracy and democratic-type governance in many parts of the world, an increasing tendency towards transparency of government and open relationships between state players, as well as a growing interest and awareness of international affairs among publics, drives the need for a more "public-aware" approach to politics, diplomacy and international relations.

2 The growing power of the international media, driven by a more informed and news-hungry audience and more influential non-governmental organizations, makes it harder for states to persist in secretive, unethical or authoritarian behaviours.

3 The falling cost of international travel, the rising spending power of a growing international middle class and its constant search for new experiences compels more and more places to market themselves as tourist destinations; at the same time, the threat of "product parity" amongst such destinations makes a clear, distinctive and economically sustainable brand strategy essential so that they can compete effectively in the international marketplace.

4 An ever more tightly linked global economic system, and a limited pool of international investors being chased by a growing number of industrial and service locations, applies similar pressures to the business of foreign direct investment promotion; again, the tendency towards parity between the offerings, and the need for a competitive strategy that is sustainable in the long term against the threat of highly mobile global capital, drives places towards an ever more sophisticated and brand-led approach to developing, managing, positioning and promoting themselves in the marketplace.

5 A range of consumer products sourced from an ever wider pool of countries increases the need to build trust in both company and country of origin; at the same time, a growing interest, reflected in the international media, in the ethical and ecological credentials of manufacturers and service providers creates a situation where it is even more critical for places to pursue a long-term strategy for building and managing positive country of origin effect.

6 For poor and developing places, the intense competition for international funds, technology and skills transfer, inward investment, export markets and trade makes a clear positioning, a well-defined sense of national economic, social and political purpose, and a degree of influence over national reputation, more and more essential.

7 Countries, regions and cities are also competing more intensely and more widely than ever before for talented immigrants, whether these are foreign nationals in search of ideal social, cultural, fiscal and living conditions, or returning members of the diaspora looking to reinvest in their home country. Again, a clear positioning, a believable and attainable set of promises in these areas, and a well-maintained and well-deserved reputation become essential attributes of the competitive nation.

8 A growing demand on the part of consumers for an ever wider, richer and more diverse cultural diet, enabled and stimulated by the rapid growth of low-cost global digital communications means that the global marketplace is open as never before for places with unusual and distinctive traditional or invented cultural products to "punch above their weight" in world affairs, and use their culture to communicate more of the real richness of their society to ever more distant audiences.

9 The currently depressed popularity of American culture, policies, products and services will create a vacuum in the global marketplace for clearly positioned and consistently presented places to build real competitive advantage.

The list could continue for page after page. The common driver of all these changes is globalization: a series of regional marketplaces (and by marketplaces I mean not just markets for products or funds, but for ideas, for influence, for culture, for reputation, for trust and for attention) which is rapidly fusing into a single, global community. Here, only those global players – whether they are countries, cities, regions, corporations, organizations, religions, NGOs, charities, political parties or individuals – with the ability to approach a wide and diverse global marketplace with a clear, credible, appealing, distinctive and thoroughly planned vision, identity and strategy can compete.

Some people claim that such a situation unfairly favours places with the funds to promote themselves more loudly than others, but that is assuming that Competitive Identity can be built in the same way as commercial brands, and that success ultimately depends on how much money you have to spend on media. I argue that this isn't so, and that a powerful and imaginative CI strategy, which is more the product of intellectual than of financial capital, can prove to be a greater asset than huge amounts of money used to thrust uninspiring messages onto an unwilling audience.

For places to achieve the benefits that the better-run companies derive from marketing and branding, the whole edifice of statecraft needs to be jacked up and underpinned with some of the lessons and techniques that commerce, over the last century and more, has acquired. Much of what has served so well to build shareholder value can, with care, build citizen value too; and citizen value is the basis of good governance today.

The need for standards

If we were speaking of nothing more than the effect of the application of marketing techniques on policy making and economic development, we would be sure of adding a much needed dose of practical, rigorous, egalitarian, good-humoured and quick-witted humanism to an area where such qualities are all too often entirely absent; but we are talking of brand management, and the consequences are far more significant. It is the creation and management of brand equity that has so changed and accelerated business during the last hundred years, and it is the creation and management of brand equity that will utterly change the way in which places develop and compete during the next hundred.

Since the combination of brand theory, public diplomacy and other forms of national promotion is such a potent tool for competitive advantage, it is essential to establish through debate and discussion the core issues of good practice, ethics and standards in the field.

Standards are urgently required because the idea that nations can be "branded", as I mentioned in the Introduction, is being taken far too literally in many places, and you don't need to speak to many national, regional or civic administrations before a pattern begins to emerge. The politicians or civil servants hear that "having a brand" is the latest thing; but they are forgivably confused about the distinction between its outward signs in the commercial context (such as slogans and logos) and the complex underlying strategy and long-term behavioural change which ought to underpin such ephemera; they start to believe that if only they could raise a Nike-sized marketing budget, then their country could have a Nike-sized brand within months.

In this way, they fall easily into the hands of the media sales people and the marketing firms. These firms, perhaps despairing of selling difficult, invisible, long-term strategic advice to politicians with a four-year event horizon, all too often revert to "selling the client what s/he wants". So what the client gets is a slogan and a logo, or a series of television spots, with nothing much behind it, and probably very little connection between it and the nation's long-term development plans. There is usually too little political will or clout for it to be sustained or taken seriously, too little investment for it to become properly established in the minds of the "audience", little understanding of who this audience actually is, or what its current perceptions of the nation brand are, and very little real coordination or common purpose between the nation's stakeholders. The list of common failings could go on, but the fact is that undertaking a national strategy that will actually make a positive difference to the way in which the place is perceived – even internally, let alone by the rest of the world – is a major long-term undertaking, and there are no short cuts to it.

The consequences of these superficial transactions between places and marketing and media firms are more serious than just another country or city or region wasting money it cannot readily afford, or creating slightly more confusion about what the place actually stands for: it is reinforcing the popular notion that brand management is synonymous with creating a visual identity or a promotional campaign, and swells the numbers of disappointed administrations that have "tried branding" and, after spending money without seeing any results, reach the conclusion that it doesn't work.

This is a great pity, because an understanding of how brand management works can create significant improvements in the way that nations develop and how they relate to each other. It is important that people properly understand what brand management is, and what it can and can't achieve for countries, cities and regions.

Most importantly, the message needs to be clearly communicated that "brand" is really just a metaphor for how countries can compete more effectively in the modern age, and that only a tiny handful of the principles of commercial branding actually apply to places. The rest is entirely new: an emerging synthesis of public and private sector theory and practice that could, and should, revolutionize the way that places are run in the future.

CHAPTER 2

The Theory of Competitive Identity

Where national reputation comes from

Most countries communicate with the rest of the world, and so deliberately or accidentally create their reputation through six natural channels.

1 Their tourism promotion, as well as people's first-hand experience of visiting the country as tourists or business travellers. This is often the loudest voice in "branding" the nation, as the tourist board usually has the biggest budgets and the most competent marketers.

2 Their export brands, which act as powerful ambassadors of each country's image abroad, but only where their country of origin is explicit: if nobody knows where a product comes from, then it can't affect their feelings about that country, but when its provenance is strongly branded, such as Mercedes (Made in Germany) or Sony (Made in Japan) or Red Stripe (Made in Jamaica), it can speak just as loudly as tourism campaigns.

3 The policy decisions of the country's government, whether it is foreign policy that directly affects overseas populations, or domestic policy that gets reported in the international media.

4 For business audiences, the way the country solicits inward investment, recruitment of foreign talent and students, and expansion into the country by foreign companies.

5 Through cultural exchange and cultural activities and exports: a world tour by a sports team, the recordings of a famous musician, the works of poets and authors and film-makers. Even a cultural product as lightweight as *Crocodile Dundee* or *Madagascar* can play a role in building the reputation of a nation, whether for better or worse.

6 The people of the country themselves: the high-profile leaders and media and sports stars, as well as the population in general; how they behave when abroad and how they treat visitors to their countries.

Figure 2.1   The hexagon of Competitive Identity

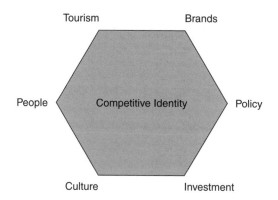

Source: Simon Anholt, *Brand New Justice* (Oxford: Butterworth Heinemann, 2003)

For clarity, I have always shown these "natural" channels of national behaviour and national communication as the points of a hexagon (see Figure 2.1).

The basic theory behind Competitive Identity is that when governments have a good, clear, believable and positive idea of what their country really is, what it stands for and where it's going, and manage to coordinate the actions, investments, policies and communications of all six points of the hexagon so that they prove and reinforce this idea, then they stand a good chance of building and maintaining a competitive national identity both internally and externally – to the lasting benefit of exporters, importers, government, the culture sector, tourism, immigration, and pretty much every aspect of international relations.

As I said earlier, most countries don't work like this, and are more like crabs in a basket. Apparently, Jamaican crab fisherman discovered centuries ago that they can leave the crabs they have caught in a basket all day long without worrying about whether they will escape: they could get out of the basket quite easily if they helped each other, but this is something that crabs will never do. All of the stakeholders in most countries pursue their own business interests and communicate their own image of the country quite independently of each other, and in consequence the country presents no clear and coherent image of itself to the outside world: it is complex, muddled and contradictory, and so never really moves forwards.

Not only do all the stakeholders in most countries operate independently of each other; they also promote their "products" (such as investment opportunities, tourism, cultural events and so forth) in a way that doesn't take into account the deliberate *capture* and *accumulation* of reputational value. Ordinary promotion, when it's carried out with no particular long-term national strategy in mind apart from growth, is an endless cycle which may or may not lead to economic development in the longer term. Unlike proper brand management, it's about *selling* the country to companies and investors, selling holidays to tourists, selling the government's policies to voters and the media and foreign publics, selling culture, selling heritage, and so on. It can be effective, but unless it's directed and driven by an underlying brand strategy, there is little chance that the country as a whole will acquire any substantial brand equity.

Every act of promotion, exchange or representation needs to be seen not as an end in itself but as an opportunity to build the country's overall reputation; and all the bodies, agencies and organizations at each point of the hexagon have to work together, meet together, and align their behaviour to a common national strategy. Then, just as the crabs can escape from the basket, so the country can escape from the stereotype it has earned by default, and work towards an identity that is inherently competitive.

Dealing with reputation

These stereotypes that are the reputations of countries, whether good or bad, seldom really reflect the current reality of the place. A common reason for this disconnection between image and reality is simply time: a place may be changing quite quickly, but its image can lag behind by years or decades. National image is like starlight which, by the time it reaches us on Earth, is only the distant echo of an event that started and finished long before.

Part of the reason things change so slowly is because we, the public, are so attached to our beliefs: we carry on believing the same things we've always believed about places, and only change our views slowly and reluctantly. There's something comforting about those simple narratives that we all hold in our minds about places, and something has to change quite dramatically in the real world before we are prepared to alter those stories or replace them with new ones.

Most people think there's little you can do to change public opinion about a country or its people: you can blame the media, people's ignorance, globalization or history, but apparently not even the richest places on earth can change a negative stereotype once it has taken root.

However, there are a few examples which prove that the international reputation of a place really *can* be made to reflect its current reality and its future aspirations more fairly. It can even start to happen quite quickly, as long as there is a clear strategy for doing so, visionary leadership, and proper coordination between government, the public and private sector, and the community.

For developing countries trying to compete in the global economy, this is good news. Even if a country does devise and implement the perfect export strategy, the perfect foreign direct investment strategy and the perfect economic development strategy, it might still be years or even decades before the world actually gets around to revising its opinion about the place, and thus changing its behaviour towards that place.

Of course, developing countries can't afford to hang around for decades, which is why every policy decision they make needs to be informed by brand management; in this way, they are taking care of their reputation *while* they are working on making the country more competitive, and ensuring that every investment made in the country plays its full part in earning it a better, truer and more useful identity.

It is both possible and legitimate for such countries to make themselves famous for what they are *going* to be, instead of what they *have* been.

The benefits of Competitive Identity

Building Competitive Identity needs clearly stated and properly agreed goals. It is quite possible to set a mixture of precise, shorter-term goals (such as a certain increase in foreign direct investment or the hosting of a prestigious international event) and longer-term changes in national image, which might be decades away. Countries with a Competitive Identity should find:

- clearer domestic agreement on national identity and societal goals
- a climate where innovation is prized and practised

- more effective bidding for international events
- more effective investment promotion
- more effective tourism and business travel promotion
- a healthier "country of origin effect" for exporters of goods and services
- greater profile in the international media
- simpler accession into regional and global bodies and associations
- more productive cultural relations with other countries and regions.

That sounds like a lot to be asking for, and it is. But *without* a Competitive Identity, few of these aims are possible at all.

Competitive Identity, like a magnet, has three properties: it attracts (consumers, tourists, talent, investors, respect, attention); it transfers magnetism to other objects (for example, a little of the magnetic appeal of Brand Italy rubs off onto Italian products and Italian people, and renders them equally attractive even when they are taken out of context); and it has the power to create order out of chaos (I am thinking of the school physics experiment where placing a magnet underneath a heap of iron filings on a sheet of paper causes the filings to arrange themselves into a symmetrical pattern).

This final property of the magnet is particularly relevant when we are discussing the administrative and organizational challenges in Competitive Identity: a powerful and attractive CI strategy can itself help to create spontaneous alignment of purpose and shared goals amongst normally competitive and even combative stakeholders.

Of course, just giving a country, city or region a new logo and a catch-phrase won't do anything to change its image or help build its future economy. As I explained in the first chapter, the reputations of places exist in the minds of hundreds of millions of consumers around the world, not on a brochure or a website or in the offices of the government or the tourist board, and just showing a few of those people some attractive designs or pelting them with slogans can't do much to change what they already believe about the place, and have believed for decades.

What's more, giving beautiful, exotic places designer logos diminishes them: it really does make them look packaged up as if they were a commercial product. No, people only change their minds about places if the people and organizations in those places start to change the things they make and do, or the way they behave.

And that's the only sense in which a nation can start to exercise some degree of control over its image: Competitive Identity is about government, companies and people learning to channel their behaviour in a common direction that's positive and productive for the country's reputation, so they can start to *earn* the reputation they need and deserve. It is the creation of a common purpose that leads to enhanced Competitive Identity both at home and abroad.

So when I talk about the relevance of brand management for countries, I'm not talking about inventing an entirely new image for them, or somehow deleting everybody's beliefs about the place and replacing them with something better. You wouldn't want to do this, you shouldn't try, and you probably couldn't even if you wanted to. But what countries can do is come up with a simple and effective strategy for making their reputation work harder for them, instead of holding them back.

The way to get to the strategy is like this:

(a) Find out how people really see the country today, and understand why this view is preventing more of them from taking an active interest in the country, respecting and admiring it, listening to what it says, investing in its economy, spending more time and money there, or whatever the particular aims of the country are.

(b) Come up with a clear vision of how people *would* need to see the country, in order for them to start doing all of these things.

(c) Work out a democratic, effective and accountable process for getting from the current brand to the future one.

Implementing Competitive Identity

To create Competitive Identity for a country, we need to understand how people's perceptions of the country are formed in the first place:

- by the things that are done in the country, and the way they're done
- by the things that are made in the country, and the way they're made
- by the way other people talk about the country
- by the way the country talks about itself.

Most people assume that the way to change the image of a country is (d): talking about yourself. In fact, this is usually the least effective and most expensive method: it costs a lot of money because using the media is so expensive, and people don't pay very much attention to it anyway because advertising is always taken with a pinch of salt. Singing your own praises isn't the best way to make other people admire you: it's better if somebody else does it for you – (c) – or, more effective still, if you can really prove your worth – (a) and (b).

The nation's reputation wasn't built through communications, and it can't be changed through communications. Building Competitive Identity isn't an advertising, design or public relations exercise, although of course these techniques are essential for promoting the things that the country makes and does: its tourist and heritage attractions, its companies and their products and services, its music and art and other cultural products, its sport, its people, its investment and employment opportunities. The quality of the marketing done by all of these stakeholders, and the consistency between the different messages they send out about the place, is an important factor in the way the place builds up its reputation; and of course good advertising often plays a major part in creating the positive tourism brands that many countries enjoy today.

That's not the same thing as a positive, famous, well-rounded national reputation, one that stimulates attention, respect, good relations and good business all around the hexagon. The fact of the matter is that each stakeholder – tourist board, investment promotion agency, corporate sector, central government and so forth – is probably not in control of all the factors that affect its business, so it is essential that they work together.

Creating more harmony between the way all of the country's companies and organizations and people do business and sell their products and services is an important part of the process of building Competitive Identity: if they are all telling the same powerful, believable, interesting story about the country, then the country has started to achieve some control over its international image.

Brand-informed policy

Getting everybody in the country to speak with one voice, and do it well, however, is just part of the solution, and on its own won't achieve any dramatic enhancement of the national image. What really makes a difference is when a critical mass of the businesses and organizations in a country becomes dedicated to the development of new things: new ideas, new policies, new laws, new products and services, new businesses, new buildings, new art, new science, new intellectual property; and when those innovations seem to be proving a few simple truths about the place they all come from, the reputation starts to move. The place produces a buzz, people start to pay attention, and prepare themselves to change their minds.

The great thing about implementing the strategy in this way is that all these actions benefit the country quite independently of their effect on its reputation: they are good for the businesses and organizations and people that carry them out, so the money invested in them is also an investment in the country's economy, rather than money simply spent on marketing communications or design, and gone forever.

I would argue that governments should never do things purely for brand-related reasons; no action should ever be conceived of or dedicated to image management or image change alone. Every initiative and action should first and foremost be done for a real purpose in the real world, or else it runs the risk of being insincere, ineffective, and perceived as propaganda (not to mention a use of taxpayers' money that is often extremely hard to justify). But there should be something unmistakable about the *way* in which these actions and initiatives are done, the style and method of their conception, selection and delivery, the context and the manner in which they are presented, and the way in which they are aligned with other initiatives, that little by little will drive the country from the image it has acquired by default towards the one it needs and deserves.

Of course, some countries may already be doing, or already have done, innovative work in many sectors, and it may even be that this work is driven by a common and widely shared national strategy. If this is the case, and if the overall image of the country still fails to live up to the reality, then the problem may be primarily one of communication: that the country simply has to get better at telling the world its story.

In the majority of cases, however, there is either too little innovation that is truly worth talking about, or else it doesn't add up to any coherent narrative, and doesn't *prove* anything about the country.

Where the notion of Competitive Identity differs from the straightforward call for more innovation (which one hears all the time and the wisdom of which nobody really doubts) is the idea of not merely stimulating more innovation, but *aligning* the innovation to a strategy for enhancing the country's international reputation. This makes the innovation more focused and more appropriate to the needs and resources of the country; and the relatively faster improvement in the country's image helps to bring in additional investment, better markets for the commercialized innovations, and more international interest and respect for the changes taking place.

In other words, brand management for countries should be treated as a *component of national policy*, not a discipline in its own right, a "campaign", or an activity that can be practised separately from conventional planning, governance, economic development or statecraft. Just as the best-run corporations see brand strategy as virtually synonymous with their business strategy, so the best-run countries should build the awareness and understanding of brand management into their policy making.

If brand management is treated as a separate discipline from statecraft, and put into a separate silo of "communications", "public affairs" or "promotion", then there is very little it can do. When, on the other hand, it becomes implicit in the way the country is run – almost, as it were, a *style of policy making* rather than a method in its own right – it can speed up change in the most dramatic way.

Competitive Identity is, you might say, the art of playing chess with reality against perception. The government has a number of pieces at its disposal for achieving national goals (some powerful, some less so), and most governments are pretty good at planning their moves and playing the market. These are the black, solid pieces that represent the reality of the country, its policies, its sectors and its various initiatives.

However, many governments don't fully realize that facing them on the other side of the board is another army, a paler, insubstantial one that represents perceptions: the way that each of their real chess pieces is actually perceived in the minds of their various audiences. That army may be arrayed in an entirely different way. What the government needs to do is to play the real, solid black pieces against the reputational ones in order to outmanoeuvre and checkmate the incorrect, outdated and negative perceptions. Sometimes, depending on how the game develops, they might be lucky and defeat a major negative perception with quite a small action, like a pawn taking a bishop: on other occasions, an apparently small but strategically important or very resilient negative or outdated belief about the country might need the expenditure of a major piece of policy or investment or innovation in order to defeat it.

The battle against perceptions isn't, of course, the only battle that governments need to play, and at the same time they are playing other games of chess against the realities of trading conditions, macroeconomics, tariffs and laws, international relations, the environment and many other factors. But the wins and losses in the game against perceptions can have effects on the country's fortunes that are most definitely real, and they have the power to enhance, accelerate, undermine or even reverse the wins and losses of the "real world".

The virtuous circle of Competitive Identity

So the first motto for the Competitive Identity project should be *actions speak louder than words.*

The second motto should be *don't talk unless you have something to say.* Marketing communications such as advertising and PR should only be undertaken when there's a good reason: something to report like a new product, an exciting initiative, an example of real innovation.

Consumers and the media aren't interested in countries talking about why they think they should be more famous, but they are usually interested in real events that are striking, relevant, and part of a bigger, compelling story.

The "virtuous circle" illustrated in Figure 2.2 shows how a nation's identity can become more competitive. It depends in the first place on having a proper competitive strategy for the country; on the creation of a culture of innovation in every sector – government, culture, tourism, business, investment promotion, education, industry – so that the country starts to produce a constant stream of new ideas, all of which serve to prove the truth of the strategy and achieve its goals. These initiatives then need to be executed impeccably, to the highest international standards: and it is here that the greatest investment needs to take place, because there is nothing more dispiriting (or bad for a country's image) than good ideas poorly executed. Then, and only then, is it time to start communicating these success stories to the world, both through the media and, wherever possible, directly to audiences around the world.

Figure 2.2   The virtuous circle of Competitive Identity

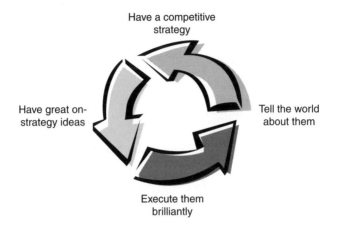

The process becomes circular and self-perpetuating because as the media become accustomed to good, new, true stories of successful innovation coming from the country, so this image begins to reinforce the reputation; the reputation, once reflected back onto the country from the international media and global public opinion generally, then inspires greater national pride, further innovation in the same and other sectors, and so it goes on.

I think it was Einstein who defined insanity as "continually repeating the same behaviour in the expectation of a different result". It is the past and current *behaviour* of the nation, region or city – or its lack of behaviour – that creates its reputation: almost every place on Earth gets the image it deserves, and imagining that one can change the image of the place without changing the way one behaves is simply naïve.

It's not that the general public is stupid or ignorant, or that the media has somehow failed to tell the truth about the place: it's usually that the country simply isn't doing enough *new things* to capture anyone's attention or prove that the place has a relevance to the lives of the people it is trying to talk to. New and interesting things are the only things that get adequately reported in the media, because they are the only things that people are always interested in:

- old boring things are very boring
- new boring things are fairly boring

- old interesting things are fairly interesting
- new interesting things are very interesting.

As long as all innovations and investments are made with the identity strategy in mind, they should all help the country to fulfil it. The more of them a country makes, and the more successful they are (in terms of their creativity, boldness and synergy with the strategy), the sooner it will improve its reputation.

If we want people to change from the story they currently believe about a country, we have to give credit to their attachment to that story. As I said earlier, they are very warmly attached to it: it is simple, credible, and functional, and it has helped them reduce the complexity of a global world, possibly for decades. They believe it because it works, and because it's interesting. There is simply no point in expecting them to voluntarily or involuntarily "trade down" from this narrative to one that's less interesting.

Clearly, innovation isn't something that you can just hope will come along: it has to be stimulated and it needs the right people and the right conditions to flourish. One of the functions of the body that manages the CI project must be to create innovation groups – if they don't already exist in the country – whose only job is to produce a constant stream of innovative ideas which can be circulated around the companies and groups and individuals that might want to add to them, combine them with their own ideas, or pick them up and give them a try.

The way they achieve this is open to discussion, but I have never agreed with the popular management creed that everyone is innately creative and the only thing that's stopping every last person in the organization from producing dozens of epoch-making ideas every day is the lack of a proper facilitator, the right leadership or management system, or the perfect environment. All my experience in both the private and public sectors has shown me that usable creativity is a faculty possessed by a small minority of exceptionally gifted people; that it is considerably sharpened by hard work and good technique; and that no technique on earth can "release" that creativity in people who don't have it in the first place. So the effectiveness of such teams is very largely to do with who their members are, and nothing much else.

Good creative ideas, it is true, are often very simple, but this is deceptive. Just because anybody can understand them or act on them doesn't mean that anybody can come up with them: in fact, quite the contrary.

In summary, creating Competitive Identity for a country, region or city is 80 per cent innovation, 15 per cent coordination and 5 per cent communication. What most places need to do is, at least in principle, nothing more complicated than this:

- decide on their identity strategy and get a good number of stake-holders behind it
- help create a new climate of innovation among those stakeholders
- show them how those innovations can really benefit their business *and* be aligned with the CI strategy at the same time
- encourage them to reflect and reinforce the identity in everything they say and do.

If it follows these steps, a country will already be managing its reputation better than most other places have ever managed to achieve.

Propaganda and Competitive Identity

If we take the virtuous circle illustrated in Figure 2.2 and try to run it in reverse, starting from the top and moving around clockwise rather than anti-clockwise, this is a pretty accurate depiction of propaganda: having a new vision for the country, and attempting to persuade people that it is already true, rather than going to the trouble and expense of doing things to prove the reality of the vision.

It is difficult to discuss the reputations of countries in any depth without such moral questions coming into the debate, and it is equally hard to discuss brand image and reputation without raising philosophical questions about reality and perception. There is a school of thought that classes a concern with popular perceptions as shallow, and somehow indicative of a basic flaw in the motivations of policy makers. According to this view, it's acceptable for the more commercial bodies – such as investment promotion agencies, tourist boards, boards of trade, and even cultural institutes – to be concerned with such superficialities as their reputation with "audiences" or "target markets", and even to expend some effort in looking after this reputation. But once we move into the arena of policy and population, there is a certain anxiety: shouldn't governments concentrate on representing the interests of the electorate, on investing in material improvements, rather than frittering away time and money in the vain pursuit of public approval?

There are several problems with this argument. First, I would claim that governments are indeed representing the interests of the electorate by building and managing the nation's Competitive Identity, as it will reap them direct benefits in terms of their employability, the desirability of the products they help to produce, the income they share from increased tourism and foreign investment, and so on. A strong country of origin effect is one of the most valuable assets that a government can help its commercial and industrial sector to create; and most importantly, the nation's reputation is the property of the people. It is *their* reputation that the government in power is temporarily safeguarding.

Second, it is in any case very hard to separate reality from perception: indeed, since we human beings only ever experience reality through our perceptions of it, it isn't difficult to argue that they are effectively the same thing. In politics as in commerce, people's perceptions of companies and policies are what really count, as they are what drive people's behaviour.

It therefore makes perfect sense to take the *reputational implications* of policy very seriously: indeed, one could argue that for a government to make investments of taxpayers' money without considering the effects this will have on the image of the country, city or region is the height of irresponsibility. To invest, for example, in hosting a major international sporting event without a proper long-term plan for capitalizing on its impact on the country's image is incompetent governance, pure and simple. Given that the nation's reputation or brand equity is one of its most valuable assets, a government must always remember its duty to the country to nurture, protect and if possible to increase that asset and leave it in better shape for its successors, even if the short-term political focus will unavoidably change from government to government.

This is an entirely different matter from choosing policies purely on the basis of their publicity value: first, because good governance always involves maintaining the correct balance between the real or ultimate value of a policy and its shorter-term image gain, and this is in no sense contradicted by the theory of Competitive Identity: indeed, the brand management focus will often provide a clearer framework for assessing and resolving such dilemmas. Second, when policies are carried out purely or primarily for their public impact, it soon becomes apparent that there is no strong underlying strategy to the behaviour, and governments that behave in this way look like leaves blowing in the wind of public opinion, and sooner or later will lose the support of their electorate: the strong underlying strategy, on the other hand, is the very basis of Competitive Identity. The right policy choice for the country's overall, long-term reputation may well be the less popular choice in the short term, so having a CI strategy is not an excuse for selecting the easier choice on every occasion.

It seems to me that what most people mean by propaganda is the deliberate manipulation of public opinion for the purpose of achieving a political end; the search for Competitive Identity is the consequence of a realization that public opinion is an essential component of achieving a political end. It is, one might say, a necessary consequence of democracy and the globalization of the media.

To go a step further, however, ask if it is legitimate for a country or city to project its *intentions* as well as the literal, current reality of the place. Can an aspirational identity strategy for a place be morally justified, in that it tells the population of the place, as well as the wider world, where the place is going?

It is certainly true that Competitive Identity aims to accelerate the "natural" lag between good actions or improved performance and the improved reputation which, in a just world, will eventually follow. A central tenet of Competitive Identity is that if the perceptual consequences of actions and behaviours are properly taken into account at the same time as those actions and behaviours are perpetrated, then the early benefits of a positive "audience response" (both internal and external) will accelerate the change. Normally it takes rather a long time for people inside and outside a place to register what is going on and which way the country is going, but when they do it causes accelerated change, mainly as a result of this common understanding leading to synergetic behaviour between the stakeholders. If this process is accelerated, then its beneficial effects can be brought forward.

It is a basic principle of Competitive Identity that places must *earn* their reputation, not construct it; but it seems perfectly legitimate (in fact, necessary) to take the trouble to look after it.

A country can behave impeccably for decades and yet still be saddled with a bad reputation which was formed long ago, and may not have been fair even then. This is quite common. National images, as I said, take a long time to form; they are made out of clichés and prejudices which sometimes seem *rusted* into place. In such cases it is obvious that the country's impeccable behaviour simply isn't being noticed, and can't be depended on to shift the negative perception. Surely the government of such a country is justified in trying to act directly on its reputation, and surely you can't call that propaganda. But who decides when the case isn't so clear-cut?

The fact is that it's enormously difficult to make people – especially people in other countries – change their minds, still less their behaviour. In the end, it's not the law or the morality of politicians that protect people from propaganda today, but the fact that the politicians probably couldn't do it if they tried, especially with a well-educated population in a modern democracy.

The influence of brand management theory on governance is probably a benign one for this reason, and to me it seems more likely to teach politicians humility than encourage tyranny. There are few better ways of learning about the intractability of human nature than trying to persuade people to spend their hard-earned money on one brand rather than another.

There's something inherently democratic about a brand-led approach to public affairs, because it's about persuasion rather than coercion, about proving rather than telling, and it's a fair contest between the public and private bodies of the state and the domestic and foreign publics (with the media and other commentators helping out). It depends a lot on rhetoric, which has always been an integral part of the democratic approach to public matters, and which is one of the main tools of marketing.

Marketing teaches that telling the truth makes good practical and commercial sense: you can only lie once. Edward R. Murrow, the legendary newsman and later one of the outstanding figures of American public diplomacy, saw the truth not only as a powerful weapon, but as an intrinsic American trait:

American traditions and the American ethic require us to be truthful, but the most important reason is that truth is the best propaganda and lies are the worst. To be persuasive we must be believable; to be believable we must be credible; to be credible we must be truthful. It is as simple as that.

Belligerent branding

I have often said that the alternative to managing national image isn't *not* managing it: it is allowing somebody else to manage it for you. This "somebody else" is most likely to be public opinion, which in the absence of anything better will always brand countries according to the most familiar and reassuring cliché, which is almost always simplistic, usually out of date, frequently rather unflattering, and occasionally extremely unhelpful. But, on occasions, the "someone else" who creates your reputation for you might actually be the government or agency of another country.

America may have lost something of its skill at managing its own brand but, when it comes to branding other countries, it is still a world leader. This it does partly through the vast economic influence of its three biggest credit rating agencies: Moody's, Standard & Poor's and Fitch. These firms dominate the world market in Sovereign Ratings, a way of grading the solvency of a country, which is used by investors the world over to decide which countries are safe to invest in, and which ones aren't. It is no exaggeration to say that the fate of nations hangs on the way these firms decide to "brand" them. To make matters worse, their conclusions are arrived at by methods which are not even published: they are considered trade secrets. In my opinion, it is high time a consortium of developing countries got together and produced an alternative measure of investment grading, perhaps based on national reputation rather than economic data because, as every marketer knows, brand strength is an excellent predictor of success in the marketplace.

America also brands other countries through the pronouncements of its leaders. Because America also owns or controls such a lion's share of the world's media, and because the utterances of US presidents are instantly reported in every corner of the world, a single well-chosen phrase can attach to a country, become massively publicized, and become extremely difficult to shake off. Ever since President Reagan fired off the epithet "Evil Empire" at the Soviet Union in 1983, it has been clear that America possesses a weapon of mass persuasion against which there is virtually no defence: I call this *belligerent branding*.

The term "rogue state" is another recent favourite of American presidents, but it has never really stuck to any country in particular (in fact, it is sometimes used against the United States by its critics). "Failed state", when used by a US president, also carries enough weight to virtually put a country out of business. An attempt to use the more politically correct phrase "state of concern" under the Clinton administration proved short-lived, presumably because there was no warhead attached.

More recently, and even more infamously, the phrase "Axis of Evil" was used by President Bush in his January 2002 State of the Union Speech. This "three for the price of one" brand has probably enjoyed more worldwide media exposure than any commercial slogan in history: within days, it was bigger than "Coke Adds Life" or "Just Do It".

It was also something a little worse than the political rhetoric or ideological exaggeration of Reagan's comment: by borrowing the term "axis" from the Axis Powers of the Second World War, Bush implied an alliance between Iran, Iraq and North Korea which suited his political aims but had little basis in fact.

Whilst these phrases may be the belligerent branding equivalent of ballistic missiles, there are also the occasional hand grenades, more often than not lobbed at friends and allies, such as "Old Europe", and the extraordinary "cheese-eating surrender monkeys" (this one was not an official federal weapon; it was coined by an American journalist and given worldwide airplay anyway).

One wonders what Arthur Miller would have thought about these tags had he been alive to witness them. Looking back at the way the US changed post-war allegiances and alliances with such insouciance, the author of *Death of a Salesman* wrote in 1987:

> It seemed to me in later years that this wrenching shift, this ripping off of Good and Evil labels from one nation and pasting them onto another had done something to wither the very notion of a world even theoretically moral. If last month's friend could so quickly become this month's enemy, what depth of reality could good and evil have?

CHAPTER 3

Understanding National Image

One of the components of brand management that is most valuable to governments in creating their longer-term plans is the analysis of brand image, and this process of assessing, measuring and tracking national image and reputation – if suitably adapted for the purposes of national rather than corporate image – is a key component of the Competitive Identity strategy.

Given the growing importance of the field, it's no longer good enough to venture opinions about which nation's brand image is stronger than another, which is declining and which is on the rise; and, more importantly, it is not acceptable for governments to be spending taxpayers' and donors' money on an exercise that can't be measured, tracked, or made accountable. It was for these reasons that I launched the Nation Brands Index,[5] the first analytical study of ordinary people's perceptions of the brand images of countries.

I quoted earlier from J.P. Morgan: "A man always buys something for two reasons: a good reason, and the *real* reason." It seemed to me that there were hundreds of surveys looking at the good reasons why people might choose to invest in a certain country, buy its products, go on holiday there, respect its government or take an interest in its culture and heritage, but nothing that explained the *real* reasons: those instantaneous, emotional, deep-rooted good or bad feelings that we all have about places. In short, there was plenty of information about what ought to go on in people's heads but nothing to tell us what goes on in their hearts.

So each quarter I poll a sample of the 5 million consumers in the worldwide online panel run by Global Market Insite in Seattle, and track their perceptions of the cultural, political, commercial and human assets, investment potential and tourist appeal of 36 developed and developing countries. This adds up to an index of national brand power, a barometer of global preference. The ranking of the top ten countries in the final 2005 survey were as shown overleaf.

Overall rank order
(3rd edition results in brackets)

1	(1)	United Kingdom
2	(5)	Switzerland
3	(9)	Canada
4	(6)	Italy
5	(7)	Sweden
6	(2)	Germany
7	(4)	Japan
8	(8)	France
9	(12)	Australia
10	(3)	United States

In the last quarter of the 2005 survey, with the help of Brand Finance, we added a new dimension to the Nation Brands Index: a financial valuation of 32 of the nation brands in the list. For the first time, it became possible to put a dollar value on the reputations of the countries in the NBI, giving a sense of the real contribution of the brand to the nation's economy. The results are given in Table 3.1.

To perform the valuation of each country brand, we used the "royalty relief" approach. This approach assumes a country does not own its own brand and calculates how much it would need to pay to license it from a third party. The present value of that stream of hypothetical brand contribution payments represents the value of the brand.

The "royalty relief" methodology is used for two reasons: first, it is the valuation methodology favoured by tax authorities and courts in many countries because it calculates brand values by reference to documented, third-party transactions; and second, because it can be performed on the basis of publicly available financial information. This method of valuing the top country brands also ensures that the results are directly comparable year on year.

Many of these figures represent a value to the economy of their country well in excess of GDP, just as the brand values of corporations often exceed their tangible assets. The valuations range from the remarkable figure of nearly $18 trillion for "Brand America" to $43 billion for "Brand Poland". It certainly adds a new dimension to the observation I

Table 3.1 Financial valuation of nation brands

Country	Brand value (US$ Bn)	Brand value/ GDP 2004 (%)	BV per head of population (US$)	Brand rating
USA	17,893	152	60,963	AA−
Japan	6,205	133	48,566	A
Germany	4,582	167	55,449	BBB+
UK	3,475	163	58,492	BBB+
France	2,922	143	48,714	BBB+
Italy	2,811	167	48,821	BBB+
Spain	1,758	169	38,566	BBB+
Canada	1,106	111	34,669	BBB
Australia	821	133	40,785	BBB
Netherlands	792	137	48,762	BBB
Denmark	772	320	143,055	BBB
China	712	43	549	BBB−
Russia	663	113	4,641	BBB−
Switzerland	558	156	75,621	BBB−
Belgium	456	130	43,864	BB+
Sweden	398	115	44,309	BB+
Norway	276	110	60,151	BB−
South Korea	240	26	4,986	BB−
Turkey	189	63	2,635	B+
Portugal	189	112	18,067	B
Brazil	181	30	1,013	B
Singapore	106	100	24,761	B
New Zealand	102	106	25,132	B
South Africa	94	44	2,282	B
Hungary	78	77	7,699	B
Egypt	67	21	976	B
Czech Republic	55	51	5,379	B
Argentina	55	36	1,432	B−
Poland	43	18	1,138	CCC

made in the first edition of the Nation Brands Index that "protecting and enhancing the nation brand, this most valuable of assets, is surely one of the primary responsibilities of governments in the 21st century".

Having now run the Nation Brands Index each quarter for nearly two years, it is pretty clear what kind of country has powerful brand values: a stable, liberal, democratic Western state with a tendency to neutrality, often producing several well-known branded products, and a strong international presence in the media (either through entertainment and culture or through attractive tourist promotion). The countries with the best brands are rich countries, too: the top fifteen countries in the NBI each have a gross domestic product of at least $23,000 per capita, whereas the bottom ten all fall below $19,000.

Countries like Canada, Australia, New Zealand and Switzerland appear to carry much of the same appeal that put Sweden at the top of the first Nation Brands Index – indeed, our panel seems to consider Australia, Canada and Switzerland as "more Swedish than Sweden".

But the world's love for Australia and Canada is, in some senses, beyond reason – or certainly quite hard to account for in practical terms. Unlike Sweden or Germany or Italy, neither country is associated with loved and world-famous commercial brands; unlike Britain, neither has any internationally prominent or respected political figures; neither is an especially prolific or prominent contributor of cultural offerings on the world stage. But both are large, beautiful, relatively remote countries with relatively small populations; they both have a certain exotic appeal which is helped by the fact that not many people are as intimately familiar with them as, say, Spain, France or America.

It's certainly easier for countries that are not in the mainstream of global politics to achieve good brand rankings: negative brand attributes nearly always accrue to first-world countries as a result of unpopular foreign policies (America's foreign policy being a case in point), and any country that regularly plays a key role in world affairs will find this kind of negative equity hard to avoid completely.

The UK is the exception that proves the rule: it is the only country in the top five of the NBI to occupy the international political and economic mainstream (it's the only trillion-dollar economy, the only permanent member of the UN Security Council, and the only nuclear power in the NBI Top Five). To maintain such a positive image despite these factors – and despite having been an imperial power within living memory – is quite an achievement.

When nation brands change

One of the main reasons why I decided to carry out this survey quarterly, at least in the early years of the Nation Brands Index, was to test out my hypothesis that if you are really testing national brand image – rather than, say, public opinion – then the results should be extremely stable, and indeed shouldn't change by more than a few percentage points here and there during the year. The real rate of change, when there is change, would be over years rather than months. Sure enough, with a few rare exceptions, we have found that from quarter to quarter, very little changes – and we are asking different consumers each time.

In my experience, the images of countries only ever change for two reasons: either because the country changes, or because it *does something* to people.

The first kind of change is, as I mentioned earlier, a gradual process, and the majority of "success stories" about brand change aren't stories of brand management at all: Ireland's change from a collapsing rural backwater in the 1960s to the "Celtic Tiger" of the 1990s was primarily a miracle of foreign direct investment promotion; South Africa's change from a virtual pariah to the "Rainbow Nation" of today was first and foremost a political miracle, triggered by the end of apartheid, the election of Nelson Mandela, one of the most innovative constitutions created in the last century. In both cases, the Competitive Identity of the country was built through its actions and behaviours, and not through any deliberate attempt to market the country directly.

The prominent marketing campaigns carried out by South Africa may have helped a little to shorten the lag between reality and global perception, by supporting what was in the news media to bring the changes to people's attention, and help summarize and characterize them. In such cases, marketing communications can certainly play a role: but it does seem to confirm that all it can really do is capture the *zeitgeist*, and reflect changes in society that are already taking place. Communications cannot substitute change, but they can report it, help to consolidate it, and to some extent speed it on its way.

Japan provides the last century's best example of enhanced Competitive Identity. The effect of Japan's economic miracle on the image of the country itself was quite as dramatic as its effect on the country's output: 40 or even 30 years ago, "Made in Japan" was a decidedly negative concept, as most Western consumers had based their perception of Japan on their experience of shoddy, second-rate products flooding the marketplace. The products were cheap, certainly, but they were basically worthless.

In many respects, the perception of Japan was much as China's has been in more recent years.

Yet Japan has now become enviably synonymous with advanced technology, manufacturing quality, competitive pricing, even of style and status. Japan, indeed, passes the best branding test of all: whether consumers are prepared to pay more money for functionally identical products, simply because of where they come from. It's fair to say that in the 1950s and 1960s, most Europeans and Americans would only buy Japanese products because they were significantly *cheaper* than a Western alternative; now, in certain very valuable market segments such as consumer electronics, musical instruments and motor vehicles, Western consumers will consistently pay *more* for products manufactured by previously unknown brands, purely on the basis that they are perceived to be Japanese. Little wonder that Dixons, a UK retailer of consumer electronics, called its new house brand Matsui (the name of a Japanese baseball player), in order to borrow a little of the "public domain" equity of Brand Japan.

Again, though, the change in the image of Japan over the second half of the twentieth century wasn't primarily designed as an image change: it was an export, design, technological and industrial miracle. South Korea, and more recently China, have quite deliberately followed Japan's lead in this but, with the advantage of hindsight, they are dealing with the image simultaneously with the product change, and using brand management techniques to build their corporate and national reputations as they build their "product" (which is why they are getting there faster).

The second reason why the images of countries change is not when things happen *to* the country, but when people are personally affected *by* the place in some way. In such cases, national reputation can change quite suddenly in the minds of certain individuals or groups.

This can be a positive change: in the Nation Brands Index data, I have found a statistically significant correlation between a positive experience of visiting a country and positive feelings about its products, its government, its culture, its people. More research is needed in this area, but an interesting hypothesis to work with at this point would be that *any positive experience of a country, its people or its productions tends to create a positive bias towards some or all aspects of the country.*

On the other hand, of course, it can be negative. A direct attack on the individual's self, country, values, religion or population, whether real or perceived, can damage the brand in that individual's mind in an equally powerful way: the most striking example of this since the Nation Brands Index started was the impact of the Danish Cartoon Crisis.

In December 2005, an international furore broke over the publication of satirical cartoons depicting the Prophet Muhammad in Denmark's *Jyllands-Posten* and other newspapers, which eventually resulted in rioting and numerous deaths, as well as widespread boycotting of Danish and other Scandinavian goods in shops all over the Muslim world. A serious rift appeared to have opened up between the values of Islam and some aspects of secular liberal Western democracy.

The first quarter (Q1) survey of the 2006 Nation Brands Index gave us an opportunity to test public feelings in the immediate aftermath of these events, and above all to see how far the overall national reputations of Denmark and other countries implicated in the cartoons controversy had shifted as a result.

Denmark and Norway had been included in the Nation Brands Index (NBI) for the first time in the last quarter of 2005, just before the cartoons were published. I wasn't sure how they would perform in relation to Sweden, which had proved over the previous year to be a highly and almost universally admired nation brand. I had a suspicion that when respondents from outside Europe answered questions about Sweden in previous editions, many of them had a kind of pan-Scandinavian or Nordic composite in their minds and were really thinking of the whole region when they answered questions about Sweden. But once our panellists were given the opportunity to score these three countries separately, it turned out that most of them were quite clear about Denmark and Norway being different from Sweden, and relatively weaker, too.

In the Q4 study, Norway and Denmark remained in level positions almost throughout the index, suggesting that many people, especially beyond Northern Europe, don't have a strong sense of the differences between these two countries, even when it comes to distinguishing between their exports (this despite the fact that Danish brands such as Lego, Bang & Olufsen, Carlsberg and several others are associated with Denmark, while Norway produces no famous global brands). The strongest component of both countries' images was in governance, where both ranked within the top five on every governance question (with Norway consistently a shade ahead of Denmark). This fitted in with a fairly well-established traditional perception – rooted, like most perceptions, in reality – that Northern European (and especially Scandinavian) countries are fairly, efficiently and liberally governed, with a strong tradition of social welfare, and a good record in international relations and development.

The NBI's coverage in Muslim countries is not yet very extensive, although it continues to develop: at the time of the 2006 Q1 survey, only four predominantly Muslim countries were included in the global panel. These were Egypt, Indonesia, Malaysia and Turkey (Turkey, although the majority of its citizens are Muslims, is of course a secular state).

Table 3.2 compares the Egyptian panel's rankings of Denmark between the last quarter of 2005 (right-hand column) and the first quarter of 2006 (left-hand column), first as overall rankings, and then by each "point of the hexagon". Denmark was relegated by the Egyptian respondents to overall last place in the survey (35th out of 35). There was been a steep decline in the Egyptian panel's ranking of Danish products (a 39 per cent drop), their association of the Danish government with the promotion of peace and security (a 34 per cent drop), their view of the Danish government's respect for the human rights and fair treatment of its own population (a 32 per cent drop), and their belief that they would be made welcome if they visited Denmark (a 30 per cent drop). Even their perceptions of Danish cultural heritage (which was put in as a neutral factor) declined by 16 per cent. One can only speculate whether these responses are typical of Arab Muslim opinion, but it seems likely that they are to some degree.

Elsewhere in the world, Denmark's scores remained more stable, although there was a slight depression in the scoring from the panellists in Central Europe (Hungary, Poland, Estonia and the Czech Republic), for

Table 3.2   Shift in Egyptian panel's rankings for Denmark

Area	2006 Q1	2005 Q4
Overall	35 (Norway 24)	15 (Norway 14)
Exports	31	19
Governance	35	7
Culture	34	20
People	35	14
Tourism	34	17
Investment	26	14

example on key questions about people's interest in Danish products and services, their expectation of being made to feel welcome if they visit the country, their propensity to employ a Dane, and their view of the Danish government's contribution to human rights and international peace and security. At the further end of the spectrum, the American panel's average scores for Denmark went up slightly (perhaps reflecting a sense of relief that for once, somebody else was in trouble).

By contrast, the Egyptian panel's average scores for China rose, which suggests that the whole axis of its global loyalties has undergone a slight shift.

Denmark was the only country in the Index that suffered a reduction in its mean overall score between 2005 Q4 and 2006 Q1.

Although some of the changes reported here are subtle, often no more than a few percentage points, they are significant because country scores generally move very little from one quarter to the next. As I mentioned before, people's views of other countries are generally quite fixed and stable, and it takes something very serious indeed to make them revise their views. Above all, it takes something *personal*.

It goes without saying that this effect can be prolonged and reinforced more or less at will from generation to generation through education and indoctrination if it is in the interests of society or government to do so, which is one reason why it is impossible to make any predictions about how long this effect will last in the case of Denmark.

Generally, if an action is strongly out of character with the nation's reputation, people's beliefs about that nation will return to their previous state relatively quickly; but it seems clear that the respect expressed by the Egyptian, Turkish, Indonesian and Malaysian respondents for Denmark prior to the cartoons episode was something that existed in one part of their being but not in another. People can hold several contradictory feelings about countries at the same time, and they can respond to surveys such as the NBI in different ways too: as consumers, as politically-aware national or global citizens, or as individuals thinking about their own lives, tastes and careers.

Given the nature of the survey, it is quite likely that in previous editions of the NBI these relatively pro-Western respondents were expressing their views about Denmark and other mature Western economies as consumers or potential consumers of their products, tourism, popular culture, employment and education opportunities, and so forth. But if Denmark touches a different nerve – a political, personal, cultural or religious one – then the reaction may temporarily or even permanently drown out what they feel for the country in other ways. We have all seen images of Coca-Cola-drinking, Nike-wearing youths in the Middle East and South Asia burning American flags.

This particular episode, like all wildfires, started in one small place, but spread rapidly because it found dry tinder and favourable winds (perhaps predictably, some people suspect arson). In consequence it soon created a violent impact well beyond Denmark's borders. As the *Arab News* reported on 28 January:

> Many international brands have become targets of the recent boycott of Danish products, thanks to the confusion of consumers caused in part by the misinformation distributed by the proponents of the ban. "The email I received said that NIDO is one of the Danish products, so I stopped buying it," said Saudi teacher Khaled Al-Harthi, who didn't know that NIDO is a product of the Swiss Nestle Company. A flier obtained by Arab News calls for boycotting Danish and Norwegian products … the flier listed many items that are not products of Denmark, including Kinder (owned by Italy's Ferrero-Rocher) and New Zealand's Anchor …
>
> Zakaria Ismail, manager of Al-Malki supermarket, said they would start hanging signs indicating Danish products. They had to do so in order to reduce their loss of sales of products that are mistaken as Danish … He said that all customers now generated the habit of reading the source of each product to make sure of its origin. "Even old people who cannot read, are asking, 'Where is this made?'" he said.

The episode is a stark illustration of the real meaning of globalization: almost every nation and culture on earth is now sharing elbow-room in a single information space. No conversation is private any longer, no media is domestic, and the audience is always global. And everybody knows what happens when a group of human beings with different backgrounds, habits, values and ambitions are thrown together in the same crowded space: sooner or later, tempers start to fray. Somebody treads on someone else's toes; some say by accident and some say on purpose; insults get traded, a fight breaks out.

The implications of the Danish cartoon episode are profound and leave us with several unanswerable questions. It is a universal human trait, whether we like it or not, to brand other countries, other races, other religions, other cultures. No matter how complex or even contradictory they are, we often resort to treating them as single entities. How quickly our disapproval of one government's foreign policy can lead to mistrust or persecution of that country's people; the failure of one company may be taken as indicative of the imminent failure of its country's economy; admiration for a single media star may lead to an imaginary liking for the entire population of the country. This case is no different: the actions of one independent newspaper are blamed on the people of the country, the government is expected to explain or resolve the issue, and the country's exporters are caught in the crossfire and their products boycotted. Even other countries have suffered because they happen to lie in the same geographical region, and have some brand values in common.

If we pursue the metaphor of national reputation as brand image, the nature of the dilemma becomes clear. Were such an episode to threaten the wellbeing and reputation of a corporation, it would be obvious what to do: the Chief Executive would address all staff, warn them that they are all equally responsible for preserving the organization's good name, and demand that they behave "on brand" or lose their jobs.

However, corporations aren't democracies: they are a species of tolerated tyranny. As the Prime Minister of Denmark Anders Rasmussen pointed out in January 2006, he is not and cannot be responsible for the behaviour of the free media in a democracy, as long as it acts within the law. Perhaps on this occasion the law was inadequate, and perhaps in an increasingly interconnected world and increasingly multiracial societies, the old models of national law need to evolve faster than they currently do. Perhaps in an enlightened modern society the forces of education, cultural sensitivity and respect could and should operate more effectively to prevent such episodes than the blunt instrument of the law.

Nevertheless, the fact remains that although countries depend on their reputations as much as corporations do, they have – quite rightly – very little power to control the way those reputations are treated or mistreated by their own citizens. Nations being viewed as single brands is a phenomenon of growing importance which is increasingly resistant to direct control, and who knows where that will lead us?

When nation brands don't change

The reputations of nations, as we have seen, are like the proverbial super-tanker which takes five miles to slow down and ten miles to change course. Aside from the two instances I've outlined here – when the country itself changes over a number of years, or when the country creates a direct and personal impact on a person or group of people – almost nothing else will divert it from its course.

It surprises many people to learn, for example, that the images of nations seem virtually immune to things that happen *to* the country, including wars, terrorist attacks and natural disasters (they are also highly resistant to even the most expensive attempts at manipulation through marketing campaigns and other propaganda). Terrorist attacks, which do temporarily create very high awareness because they are more widely and more intensely reported in the global media, appear to have little impact on the image of the country or city as a whole, even in the short term.

The terrorist attacks in Cairo, Madrid, London and of course New York and Washington may be spontaneously associated with those cities by as many as 60 per cent of the City Brands Index respondents worldwide, but London, New York and Madrid are still ranked among the top ten city brands overall; London and Madrid are even rated 11th and 12th safest cities by our panels, well above certain cities where no serious attacks have occurred or are expected (such as Milan, Prague and Hong Kong).

When the Nation Brands Index was first published, many Dutch people expressed surprise at the health of their national reputation, and asked whether the world knew nothing of the assassinations of the film-maker Theo van Gogh and the politician Pim Fortuyn. (Interestingly, there was a similar reaction in Sweden, where people were just as surprised that the murders of Prime Minister Olof Palme and more recently the Foreign Minister Anna Lindh hadn't utterly destroyed the image of Sweden.) The fact is that the reputations of the Netherlands and Amsterdam, Sweden and Stockholm, like most mature and successful brands, have long ago achieved critical mass, so that people simply reject anything negative which threatens to contradict the overwhelmingly positive "brand story" that they carry in their minds. It's too much trouble for most people to revise the things they have always believed about cities and countries just because something shocking or out of the ordinary has happened there.

Problems in places with powerful and positive reputations – even grave problems including politically or racially motivated murders – seem to be received by the world as the exception that proves the rule. A typical reaction would be "A murder in broad daylight – how shocking! Holland/Amsterdam/Sweden/Stockholm is such a safe place!" Obviously this won't last forever, and if bad news from Holland or Sweden starts to become a regular event it will eventually spoil the image. But for the time being, the positive reputation outweighs the negative events, and Stockholm and Amsterdam are still rated 2nd and 7th safest of the 30 cities in the City Brands Index.

It seems that people are better able to weigh up probabilities than psychologists sometimes give them credit for: the cities that are ranked lowest for safety in the City Brands Index tend to be the ones where everyday crime and lawlessness are highest, not the ones where an outrage has recently been perpetrated. New York languishes in 23rd place for safety and Washington in 19th, but this is more likely to be because both cities have a reputation for high levels of street crime than because of 9/11.

There's another reason why things that happen *to* a country often have a weaker impact on people's perceptions of the place than one might expect: we are all subjected to so much news and information every day that we tend to process it at a fairly low level. Much of the time, we don't observe the international news in a very alert fashion: it is a distant spectacle that, no matter how shocking, doesn't really affect us very deeply. We may not register much more than the subject of the news item, and absorb very little about what has happened there, or whether it was good or bad. More than one airline has, in the past, reported an increase in the number of its bookings immediately after a highly-publicized accident, and this isn't because we all have some kind of death-wish: it's because the brand has had a huge amount of exposure, and it is at the front of our minds. After the movie *Titanic* was released – and it was a film about a cruise ship sinking – a definite spike in the number of cruise bookings was recorded.

I call this low-level processing the "Homer Simpson effect" in hon-our of the way that Homer Simpson, slumped in front of the television, is only dimly aware of what is going on in front of him: and yet his instincts are subconsciously stimulated by what he sees. This is the reason why people are often heard to state that "all publicity is good publicity": this statement is patently untrue, but does contain a grain of truth in it. Even a natural disaster and a human tragedy on the scale of the 2004 Indian Ocean tsunami did far less damage to the images of the countries affected by it than many people expected: and this was partly due to the fact that all of them received so many hours of global exposure on television and, because of the shortage of current footage, a great deal of the film shown was library footage of the resorts *before* the disaster occurred. Within a year, most of the countries affected were quickly approaching a complete revival of their tourist numbers: there were appalling human and eco-nomic losses, but the nation brands survived, as they almost always do.

Why did they survive? Because the brand images of Sri Lanka, Thailand, or the Maldives aren't to be found in those countries: they exist in the minds of millions of consumers, scattered around the world. As I explained in the first chapter, the most valuable asset of those coun-tries, their reputation, is safely distributed in a remote, secure, distributed location.

The self-images of countries

I have already mentioned that the population's own perceptions of the nation brand are a powerful driver of the external image, the equivalent in public affairs of what corporations sometimes call "living the brand". For this reason, it is very instructive to examine how the population of the country ranks its own nation brand, and to see whether there are any links between this and the way in which other countries rank it.

In the Q3 report of the Nation Brands Index, I commented on the ten-dency of countries with powerful reputations to rate their own countries highly, and how this suggests that there may be some kind of real par-allel with "living the brand" at the national level. In the 2005 Q4 results, this phenomenon is clearer than ever: every one of the top 15 nation brands puts itself first, while only two of the bottom 20 do so (see Table 3.3).

Table 3.3   Country rankings overall, and of themselves, 2005 (Q4)

Country	Overall	Self
United Kingdom	1	1
Switzerland	2	1
Canada	3	1
Italy	4	1
Sweden	5	1
Germany	6	1
Japan	7	1
France	8	1
Australia	9	1
United States	10	1
Spain	11	1
Holland	12	1
Norway	13	1
Denmark	14	1
New Zealand	15	1
Belgium	16	3
Ireland	17	1
Portugal	18	5
China	19	n.a.
Russia	20	8
Hungary	21	10
Brazil	22	4
Singapore	23	8
Argentina	24	5
South Korea	25	5
India	26	1
Mexico	27	2
Egypt	28	13
Czech Republic	29	4
Poland	30	15
Malaysia	31	4
South Africa	32	6
Estonia	33	7
Indonesia	34	15
Turkey	35	3

Whether this is cause or effect is a fascinating and probably unanswerable question. Are the much lower self-rankings of the less powerfully branded countries simply a realistic appraisal of the country's modest assets, or are they a kind of self-fulfilling prophecy? It is noticeable that the two countries in the bottom 20 that do buck the trend and rank themselves first are also two of the fastest-growing economies: India and Ireland. Ireland lies only just outside the top 15, but India is still a long way down the list of nation brands, in 26th place. It's hard to know whether this is the cool confidence of a country destined for tremendous growth in the coming years, or simply optimism and indomitable national pride.

The Russians present a fascinating mixture of nationalistic fervour and political despair: in the third quarter of the 2005 survey, they ranked themselves top in the world for tourism, culture, people, investment and immigration climate, and even fifth in the world for the quality of their branded exports (a remarkable victory of national pride over realism, since Russia produces virtually none). Yet they ranked themselves dead last – 25th out of 25 – for governance. In short, the Russians see themselves as the best people in the world living in the best country in the world, only held back by the worst government in the world.

Almost all of our country panels rank their own people as best in the world, and there are only three exceptions to this rule: the Germans, who rank themselves fourth after the Canadians, the Swedes and the Australians; and the Poles and the French, who seem to prefer Canadians. (This love for the Canadians is, sadly, unrequited: the Canadian panellists rank France 12th and Poland 17th for their people.)

If you don't believe in your own brand, it's unlikely that anybody else will: and perhaps this is one part of the reason why Poland, despite its remarkable economic, social, industrial and political progress since the end of Communism, still languishes in the bottom quartile of the Nation Brands Index.

And there was a surprise self-ranking result in the final quarter of 2005: for the first time, the US panel didn't put its own country at the top of every point of the hexagon. In fact, American self-esteem appeared to have slipped on every aspect of the governance rankings since the previous NBI was carried out: the US panel scored itself slightly lower on the question of international environmental and ethical policy, and substantially lower on questions of domestic policy, internal human rights and fairness, and its contribution to international peace and security. The lower scores resulted in a considerable drop, from second place on international peace and security, to sixth place. On domestic human rights and fairness, the US lost first place to Canada: this is surely the exact equivalent of American tourists putting maple leaf patches on their rucksacks before going touring in Europe.

Measuring city brands

Cities are rather different from countries: they aren't usually famous for producing particular products or services, the tourism emphasis is often as much on conventions as on leisure visitors, the apparatus of government is usually more technocratic than political, and the city's culture isn't always easy to distinguish from the culture of the country as a whole.

It is always hard to generalize about a whole country, since there can be wide discrepancies in climate, culture, people and infrastructure from one region to another, but cities are simpler, smaller and easier to think of as a single entity. And when people consider cities, they often think in quite practical terms, concentrating on issues such as climate, pollution, transport and traffic, the cost of living, leisure and sport facilities, law and order, and the cultural life of the city.

Cities don't usually have a strong political aspect to their image, even when they are known to be the seat of national government; there is something of a "firewall" in people's minds between the actions of a national government and the individual cities in a country, and indeed some cities have more powerful brands than the countries in which they are situated, such as Paris and France, Amsterdam and the Netherlands, and several others. This can create problems while it lasts: the wealth created by investment, trade and tourism in a famous city doesn't always trickle down very efficiently to needier but less well branded cities and regions (as the Czech Republic has found to its cost).

For these and many other reasons, the City Brands Index[6] is based on a different hexagon from the one we use for the Nation Brands Index: see Figure 3.1 (a very similar one is used for the State Brands Index in the US, as subnational regions are in many ways analogous to cities).

The six components of the City Brands hexagon are explored in more detail below.

The presence

This point of the City Brands hexagon is all about the city's international status and standing. In this section, we ask how familiar people are with each of the 30 cities in the survey, whether they have actually visited them or not, and ask what the cities are famous for. We also ask whether

Figure 3.1 The City Brands Index hexagon

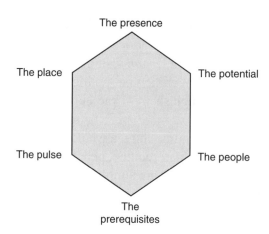

each city has made an important contribution to the world in culture, science or in the way cities are governed during the last 30 years.

The place

Here, we explore people's perceptions about the physical aspect of each city: how pleasant or unpleasant they imagine it is to be outdoors and to travel around the city, how beautiful it is, and what the climate is like.

The potential

This point of the City Brands hexagon considers the economic and educational opportunities that each city is believed to offer visitors, businesses and immigrants. We ask our panels how easy they think it would be to find a job in the city, and, if they had a business, how good a place they think it would be to do business in. Finally, we ask whether each city would be a good place for they themselves or other family members to get a higher educational qualification.

The pulse

The appeal of a vibrant urban lifestyle is an important part of each city's image. In this section, we explore how exciting people think the cities are, and we ask how easy people think it would be to find interesting things to do, both as a short-term visitor and as a long-term resident.

The people

The people make the city, and in this point of the hexagon we ask whether our respondents think the inhabitants would be warm and friendly, or cold and prejudiced against outsiders. We ask whether they think it would be easy for them to find and fit into a community which shares their language and culture. Finally, and very importantly, we ask how safe our panellists think they would feel in the city.

The prerequisites

This is the section where we ask people about how they perceive the basic qualities of the city: what they think it would be like to live there, how easy they think it would be to find satisfactory, affordable accommodation, and what they believe the general standard of public amenities is like (schools, hospitals, public transport, sports facilities, and so on).

In the first City Brands Index, London took the top position, followed by Paris, Sydney, Rome and Barcelona. These and the other rankings are shown in Table 3.4.

The City Brands Index shows that cities, just like countries, have images that rise and fall very slowly, and this is a double-edged sword. On the one hand, it means that cities in developing countries find that their new prosperity and opportunities can take an age to pass into widespread international awareness; but, on the other hand, it does mean that cities with positive brands are surprisingly immune even to catastrophic events. And once or twice in a generation, a city such as Sydney or Dubai manages to prove that a meteoric rise to celebrity and popularity can occasionally occur.

When the image of a heavily promoted city does change for the better, a closer look reveals that, just as we have found with countries, the advertising and marketing didn't achieve the change: what they did was to reflect a *real* change that was taking place in the conditions, the people, the policies and the opportunities of the city, and perhaps help the world to realize and to understand those changes a little faster and a little more fully than they would otherwise have done.

Table 3.4   Results of the first City Brands Index

City	Rank
London	1
Paris	2
Sydney	3
Rome	4
Barcelona	5
Amsterdam	6
New York	7
Los Angeles	8
Madrid	9
Berlin	10
San Francisco	11
Toronto	12
Geneva	13
Washington	14
Brussels	15
Milan	16
Stockholm	17
Edinburgh	18
Tokyo	19
Prague	20
Hong Kong	21
Singapore	22
Rio de Janeiro	23
Beijing	24
Mexico City	25
Moscow	26
Johannesburg	27
Cairo	28
Mumbai	29
Lagos	30

That is a useful task to have performed, even if the costs of achieving it effectively and sustainably are too high for many cities to justify. What advertising and marketing can't ever do is to make a bad city look good: once again, that's propaganda, not brand management, and it's as wasteful as it is ineffectual.

CHAPTER 4

Planning for Competitive Identity

What is it that makes the government of a country, a city or a region decide it needs to improve its reputation? I have yet to come across a place that's actually happy with its image (although much of this discontent is, to borrow A. H. Maslow's definition,[6] the "low grumbles" of countries with highly-developed economies and correspondingly highly-developed expectations).

Probably the most common of these grumbles is that the image of the place is outdated and no longer useful for supporting its economic, political or developmental goals: but since the reputations of places naturally evolve at a very slow rate, this is an almost universal problem. Indeed, one of the most common reasons for developing a Competitive Identity, especially for developing countries, is simply to prevent the image of the place from lagging too far behind its fast-changing reality.

In reality, an outdated image can only mean one thing: that people haven't heard anything more interesting coming out of the country than the last interesting thing that happened there. And if the last interesting thing that happened there was beyond living memory, it means that the place has no identity beyond its immediate neighbourhood – unless, of course, the event in question was so important that it is still remembered by ordinary people in other countries and not just historians (for example, Hiroshima, Waterloo, Krakatoa, Carthage or Kitty Hawk).

It is no accident, however, that these are usually cities, towns or villages, not countries: unforgettable historical events (and they are usually battles or disasters) tend to brand their exact locality, not the country in which that place happens to lie. Too many other things happen in countries for them to be famous for one event, and time generally clouds over the associations. But small places that are plucked from anonymity by epoch-making events, and then settle back into normality, can remain branded for centuries by that one event.

Whatever the reason given, the governments (and often the people too) of most places appear to believe that there is a problem of some sort with their international image, but sometimes too little effort is expended on further identifying and analysing that problem. The idea that a country has a negative reputation becomes a commonplace, part of the "groupthink", and governments often race off to find a solution before the problem has been properly understood.

It's a fundamental premise of any strategic task to be highly specific about the nature of the problem so that the right strategy can be developed for dealing with it. It's also very important to make quite sure that there *is* a problem, and it's not simply an unfounded perception on the part of the country itself. Reading the domestic media in the United Kingdom, for example, it is clear that commentators from all political persuasions are convinced that Britain's international image is in shreds and tatters as a consequence of foot and mouth disease, mad cow disease, the invasion of Iraq, the terrorist bombs in London, the high cost and low standards of its public transport, and so forth: yet the Nation Brands Index shows that Britain is in fact one of the most highly-regarded nations on the planet.

And the first and most important question that any country needs to ask itself is to what extent its undesired reputation is deserved. The reputations of countries aren't entirely invented by public opinion: at some stage, the country has usually done things, or failed to do things, that created the reputation. This kind of objectivity is important because it's essential to know whether the poor reputation is genuinely unfair, and purely the result of a gap between reality and perception – in which case the problem may be largely a communications problem, and communications can play a major role in fixing it – or whether the poor reputation is deserved, in which case new policies and new behaviours are the only answer.

Dealing with an information gap

If the problem with the country's reputation is indeed an information gap, and the negative image genuinely undeserved, governments should beware the trap of believing that information gaps can be filled with information. We live in an information age, and it's not very likely that the "missing" information about the country and its achievements is unavailable to the public. The reason why people don't know about the latest achievements of the country is probably not that they looked for the information and couldn't find it: it is almost certainly because they never felt inclined to look for it. Simply producing more websites and brochures is highly unlikely to cure this problem. People need to be stimulated to learn about places; they cannot be taught about them. This is the job of marketing, not information provision. Marketing is a kind of adult education; it's the way in which people continue to be persuaded to acquire new information after they have reached adulthood and can no longer be stuffed with it against their will.

Information provision and marketing are very different things, and the distinction between the two is often not well understood in government circles. Information provision is passive or "permission-based" marketing, because it has no intention and no power to impose itself on people or change their minds. If it's well produced it can have some persuasive power, but unless it is requested by a consumer it won't get the opportunity to attempt persuasion. People welcome informational materials when they are actively in search of information, and this is almost always when they have already made their mental shortlist and decided to buy. In fact the information is often sought *after* they have bought: research shows that car brochures are very often read by people who have just bought that same brand of car, simply reassuring themselves that they have made the right decision. The same may well be true of holiday brochures and investment promotion prospectuses.

Information has little value in the modern world because there is so much of it. Thanks to the Internet and the explosion in periodical publication, free newspapers, customer magazines, satellite television, digital radio, direct marketing and so on, we are all drowning in information. So we are less and less willing to pay any attention to it: the value of words and images has been reduced virtually to zero. Indeed, information not only has no value, it has a considerable cost: it costs the producer of the information to produce and present it, and it costs the consumer time and attention to absorb it.

Between them, the various stakeholders in national governments produce an enormous amount of information material, much of which is helping their business (and the nation's overall reputation) even less than passive marketing usually does, because the quality of the design and production is too low, or there is too much contradiction between the different points of the hexagon. If it were possible to pool all the money being spent on information materials by different bodies and agencies in a country, and spend it instead on proper advertising campaigns to increase tourism and foreign investment, there might be a real and fairly swift benefit. Of course the expense is considerable, and it has to be maintained: there's no point in advertising at a frequency that's too low to achieve recall, or just for a season, or even just for a year. If you inflate the country's image "artificially" with advertising, it's essential to keep it inflated while the target market and its loyalty build up to sustainable levels.

I very seldom advise places to spend money on conventional marketing: in fact I more often find myself persuading them not to, because the money is usually better spent on genuine improvements to the place which will also have a more powerful, more credible and longer-lasting effect on its reputation. Places, in the end, are not products on sale to a consumer, and traditional product marketing is usually completely unsuited to the task. But if, after careful and objective analysis, it can be clearly shown that the country has really been hiding its light under a bushel, then *marketing the information* to the audience – in other words, persuading them to absorb the information rather than simply pushing it towards them – may be part of the answer.

Analysing the Competitive Identity task

It's important for countries to distinguish between negative reputation that matters, and negative reputation that can be safely ignored because it has no consequences.

Governments may pour considerable resources into attempting to improve their country's image in another country where it is held in low esteem: but if this country is not an important trading partner, or likely to become one in the near future, or it does not have significant influence over other nations which are important partners, or significant influence over international opinion in general, and is not an important ally or source of talent or partner in cultural relations or the home country of a significant diaspora, then the motivation to "fix the image" is mere vanity or hurt pride; and salving hurt national pride is not usually a valid motive for spending taxpayers' money.

So the first stage of the CI programme must be to take a good look at the current image of the place, and to make an assessment of exactly how and why it needs to be changed. Different places need to work on their reputations for different reasons:

1. If the place is simply unknown to its target market, then it needs to be *introduced*, obviously concentrating on the sectors where it can deliver efficiently, profitably and sustainably.
2. Some places are known, but to "wrong" audiences that can't help the place fulfil its ambitions (for example, people with too little or too much spending power). Here, the country's reputation needs to be *targeted* more accurately to the right countries, regions or cities, or to new demographic groups, business sectors or decision-makers.
3. Some places are well known, but for the wrong reasons, so the image needs to be *corrected*. There are four main types of incorrect image:

   (a) Associations that are positive, but limited or unhelpful for various reasons; here, the image needs to be *expanded* to include the attributes, benefits and offerings that are more relevant and more motivating to the marketplace.
   (b) Awareness that is so vague or generic it doesn't help the place to differentiate itself from the competition; here, the image needs to be *enhanced* with more precise, more relevant and more distinctive qualities.
   (c) Associations that are out of date and can no longer make productive connections between the current offerings of the place and its current audience; here, the image needs to be *revitalized.*

(d) Associations that are actually negative; here, the image needs to be *improved*, so that the audience is gradually encouraged to shift its perceptions towards the positive attributes, benefits and offerings of the place:

- if the negative perceptions are entirely unfounded, they need to be *refuted* or *suppressed*; in some cases it's simply better to ignore them; the choice will vary from case to case.
- if the negative perceptions are founded in truth, the first thing to do is address the problems and communicate that they are being addressed as soon as real progress can be demonstrated; then, the negative perceptions can either be *contextualized*, so that the audience understands them better and can keep them in a healthier balance with the positive attributes, or *de-emphasized*, so that they occupy less space in the audience's mind – again, the choice will vary from case to case.

Most places fit into several of these categories; in fact, there may well be parts of their reputation that belong in all three main groups.

The picture is further complicated by the fact that global popular opinion is far from homogeneous. Another critical piece of analysis which, surprisingly enough, governments often fail to undertake is a proper "map" of the country's key audiences for each of its sectors: trading partners, export markets, political allies, cultural partners, source countries for tourists, talent, students, business visitors and so forth. Of course each of these countries or regions must also be subjected to at least a general demographic analysis (for example, different age groups often differ widely in their perceptions of foreign countries: one of many such interesting results from the Nation Brands Index is the observation that younger, poorer and predominantly female French respondents tend to be fairly pro-American, whereas older, better-educated and richer males are more often anti-American).

The analysis may appear dauntingly complex, but this should not prevent the solution from being rather simple, which it needs to be, if it is to be clearly understood and properly absorbed by the numerous national stakeholders, and if it is to guide their behaviour in any way at all, rather than simply end up gathering dust on a shelf somewhere (as all too many of these initiatives do).

Case notes: Germany and boringness

In some cases, a negative national reputation or a negative component of that reputation might actually be more of an asset than it first appears. One such case is Germany.

The Nation Brands Index data suggests that Germany has a generally positive but somewhat unbalanced image: its governance is much admired, its investment potential well recognized, and only Japan is better regarded as a producer of goods. German people, too, are highly regarded, but as potential employees or managers rather than as friends or hosts: they come 4th for "hireability" and 15th for hospitality, implying that Germans are perceived as effective and reliable rather than fun and likeable.

However, Germany scores disgracefully poorly as a tourist destination in the NBI: it is ranked 15th, virtually at the bottom of the "safe" destinations – in fact, below two which are not usually chosen by the risk-averse (Brazil and Egypt); the adjective most often used to describe Germany's tourism offering is "predictable". Perceptions of Germany's cultural heritage are also surprisingly weak, and Germany ranks well below the countries traditionally considered by educated Europeans as its cultural peers or inferiors: Britain, France, Italy, Spain.

Overall, Germany's image appears healthy but hard and cold: it is not a nation much associated with warmth, hospitality, beauty, culture or fun. In a word, Germany is perceived in many parts of the world as little more than a factory for consumer goods and, given the rise of China, being perceived as a factory is an increasingly risky market position in the world today.

This is not the first time that research has suggested such weaknesses in Germany's image abroad. The trouble is that the people who already know and love Germany are well aware that the Germans have a wonderful sense of humour, are exquisitely hospitable, and live in a beautiful country with a rich cultural heritage; and the people who don't already know these things simply won't believe them, because they contradict the narrative they have held in their minds about Germany for years. Simply telling those people that they've been wrong in viewing the Germans as a cold, efficient, humourless race – even assuming they are listening – is unlikely to do anything much more than reinforce the prejudice.

In any case, painful though it undoubtedly is for the Germans to see their own image reflected back in this way, it may not be quite as negative as it first appears. We live in dangerous times, faced by new and previously unimaginable threats and massive political, ecological, social and economic instability. In such times, the national images that people find most attractive are the ones that seem to communicate stability, reliability, probity, integrity, trustworthiness and social justice. Nations such as Germany, Sweden, Switzerland and Canada, which are perceived to stand for these values, are treasured as still points in a turbulent world.

This suggests that Germany's attempts to update and lighten up its serious image may be ill-advised. To be considered predictable and serious-minded, even boring, is next-door to being reliable and trustworthy; and trust is one of the most scarce and precious resources in the world today. Combine this seriousness with Germany's widely accepted commitment to environmentalism and social, corporate and political ethics, and you can imagine a day when some might see Germany as the conscience of the planet.

There have also been several attempts to update the image of Germany so that it appeals to a younger audience, but this is an enormous task. Young consumers are notoriously hard to target and harder to please because they resist all attempts to be persuaded by anyone except their chosen acquaintances.

Trying to be funny probably won't work either, for the simple reason that German humour doesn't travel well. The German sense of humour – like the English – tends to be language-based but, unlike English, German is not a global language, so the quality remains unappreciated by the majority of the world's citizens.

The Germans might just have to settle for being considered a bit serious, and they can take comfort from the fact that the opposite problem is a much tougher one to deal with. The Italians and the

Brazilians find that their image as fun-loving party folk constantly frustrates their efforts to be taken seriously in business and in international relations, no matter how great their achievements in these areas.

Competitive Identity and national character are of course intimately linked, and the quirks of Germany's image are fundamentally the quirks of the Germans themselves. Like the British, albeit for different historical reasons, the Germans aren't quite sure how to love themselves, and it's a fundamental tenet of human psychology that it's hard to love somebody who doesn't quite know how to love himself. (The Italians have little trouble knowing exactly who they are and taking great pleasure in it; and the consequence – as the Nation Brands Index shows – is that almost nobody has any trouble liking them.)

Competitive Identity, like most great social enterprises, ultimately depends on visionary leadership. Germany, for good reasons, is nervous of visionary leaders, but without some clear and widely shared sense of the nation's future role in the world, it seems unlikely that the kind of benign nationalism which is a precondition of a Competitive Identity will be achieved.

Like most other countries, Germany needs to learn how to believe in itself before it can inspire belief in others.

Getting attention

Of all the qualities needed by those who are responsible for nurturing a country's image, objectivity is one of the most valuable, and one of the hardest to achieve. After all, Marketing Directors who are responsible for marketing a product are generally salaried employees, are seldom the inventor or manufacturer of the product, and so don't find it too difficult to take a cool, objective view of the brand they're building: indeed, good ones are valued precisely because of their ability to see the brand in the same way as the consumer.

However, when the product doesn't come out of a factory, but is the very homeland of the people trying to market it (where they and their parents and grandparents were born, raised, schooled and trained), and when they are public servants rather than marketing professionals, and when brand management is merged with foreign policy, public diplomacy, tourism or trade promotion, objectivity becomes an extremely elusive quality.

A lack of objectivity can be fatal to the image strategy of a country, no matter how good the intentions at the start. Typically, I find communications departments in ministries producing lists of their country's achievements and natural advantages: the nation's most distinguished sons and daughters, the role it has played in world events, its own major historical moments, gems of architecture and natural beauty, regional cuisine, language and folklore, all served up with pages of indigestible demographics and statistics about Gross Domestic Product and income per capita. The idea is that this mass of data is then distilled into a pithy slogan and a raft of quasi-tourism collateral, and thus the country is marketed to an impatient world.

From the point of view of a busy consumer halfway across the world, of course, the historical achievements and natural advantages of most countries are of little interest, and seldom add up to anything that could be described as a coherent or powerful brand. Indeed, since Competitive Identity is most urgently needed by the smaller, poorer and newer countries, it is all the more likely that such facts will seem pretty unimpressive to the detached observer. On more than one occasion, I have been faced with the tricky task of gently explaining to a very proud and very patriotic minister that the world will not be enthralled by the fact that the world's first all-metal suspension bridge was invented by a man whose grandfather came from his country, or that over 60 different species of wild grass grow along his eastern coastline.

Any kind of marketing is like trying to chat up someone in a crowded bar. You walk up to somebody you've never met, and have a few seconds to convince them that you are worth getting to know better, and to win the chance of a longer conversation. Often a joke will do the trick, but being light-hearted about their own country is one thing that most governments find hardest to do. Either way, there are few countries and few people who will fall in love with a stranger who kicks off the conversation with a long list of his natural advantages, impressive family tree and key achievements.

There is a real risk that smaller countries with limited achievements may simply confirm the world's belief that they are a smaller country with limited achievements by telling people about the handful of world-class or nearly world-class assets they have, and of which they are greatly proud. But the fact is that the potential investor, tourist or consumer is already comparing them with countries that are in a completely different league, and their expensive marketing will simply serve to emphasize the differences, to their own disadvantage.

Rather than attempt to measure themselves up against much bigger, richer or more successful countries, it is far better for countries to identify where their real genius lies, and what are their unique abilities or potential that really do put them in a class of their own. This potential may well be the result of their small size, small population or small economy, not something that they manage to achieve despite it. Most countries, if they look hard enough, will find something that is uniquely theirs, and inherently competitive.

Building the CI team

Competitive Identity is not a stand-alone programme, but a new perspective on the normal national tasks of planning, policy making and development: rather than operating alongside normal governance, it can only work if it is allowed to permeate all of these tasks.

For this reason, it is not something that can be outsourced to external agents or consultants, or moved aside into a new division or government agency. Since managing the national image is a core responsibility of national government, the measures for doing this must be incorporated into the daily business of governance, as well as into the daily business of all the major stakeholders of national reputation: look back at the points of the hexagon, as described in Chapter 2.

So the task of "implementing" Competitive Identity is more than anything else a retraining or coaching task: all the key players need to be trained in national brand management, and helped to an understanding of how this affects their usual activities.

Building a Competitive Identity is simply too important a task to be left to government alone, however; it's too important to be left to business; and it's too important to be left to civil society. Only a carefully managed coalition of all three can undertake the task, and manage it in the long term.

It is also a project that needs the personal backing and commitment of the head of government and the head of state too, because unless responsibility for the nation's reputation is clearly taken by the highest public servants, it simply will not be seen by others as enough of a priority for the job to be effectively undertaken; and also because strong and visionary leadership is a necessary component of the project.

Building and maintaining the Competitive Identity of a country is an ongoing national project, and there are four basic qualities which I see as the essential motivations for the people who manage the process.

These qualities are rather simple and rather old-fashioned: they are wisdom, patience, imagination and care.

1 *Wisdom* is essential because it's often very hard to make the right choices between short-term promotion and long-term image management, especially when there is immediate economic pain.

2 *Patience* is necessary because the reputations of places move very slowly. The reputation that one inherits today may be the cumulative effect of centuries of management and mismanagement, some of it deliberate and most of it not. It will certainly take years, if not decades, to change it.

3 *Imagination* is important because only innovation and creativity can create real progress, change the reputation and keep it healthy. "Management" is a dull word indeed for what places really need, but there must always be a proper balance between the creative spark and the steady hand on the tiller. This balance must be reflected in the team that takes responsibility for managing the CI process.

4 *Care* is important because only people who have the best interests of the country at heart can be trusted always to do the right thing for its ecology, economy and community. One can rearrange the order of those three words endlessly, trying to put them in the right order, but in fact there is no right order: all three of them have exactly equal priority, and the key to managing the reputation of the country is

to create a structure that is able and willing to hold these three in equilibrium.

Developing the identity; developing the strategy

Where does the vision for Competitive Identity come from, the "brand strategy" or unique positioning that the country needs to work towards?

My choice of the word "identity" to describe this process is a deliberate one, because it has much in common with national identity. Here is one of the most important distinctions between the way brand management works in the commercial sphere and in the context of nations, cities and regions: you can't simply make up the brand of a place, because it almost invariably has one already. When devising a new corporate or product brand, the start of the process is often a team of creatively minded individuals dreaming up a brand strategy that is designed to be unique, aspirational, responsive to consumer needs, and inherently competitive in the marketplace.

Countries couldn't be more different. A phrase I often use when talking about Competitive Identity is "the people are the brand – the brand reflects the genius of the people". This is because it is the people and their education, abilities and aspirations that ultimately make the place what it is, and create the potential for tourism, business, cultural and social and political exchange. Without some sense of the people and their particular nature and ability, a place is just an empty landscape.

For this reason, the process of arriving at the CI strategy is more like mining than forging: it needs to be dug out of the history, the culture, the geography, the society of the place. National identity and nation brand are virtually the same thing: nation brand is national identity made tangible, robust, communicable, and above all useful. Unless the overall strategy chimes with something fundamentally true about the place and its people, there is little chance that it will be believed or endorsed by the population, let alone the rest of the world.

However, truth alone is not sufficient to make the strategy inherently competitive: as I have stressed more than once before, the world also demands that each nation's story should be interesting enough for them to pay attention to it. And if the story is a new one, it needs to be not only demonstrably true, but also significantly *more* interesting than the one it replaces.

These factors place many demands on the CI strategy, and a mistake that I frequently encounter in places looking at identity issues is the failure to establish and agree on adequate *selection criteria* for the strategy itself before embarking on the strategic process.

Without such criteria, it becomes difficult for people to agree about what's appropriate and workable for the place and what isn't; selecting ideas becomes a matter of personal taste and opinion; and when there are so many different stakeholders and different points of view, this is a recipe for slowing down or blocking the strategic process.

One example of a criteria set is a simple six-point model I use for evaluating any CI strategy or creative idea. I usually find that if an idea gets "ticks" in most or all of the parts of this model, it may not be to everybody's taste, but it will probably add something to the country's reputation and provide a return on the effort put into it.

The main purpose of these particular criteria is to ensure that the strategy is compelling and motivating – enough to drive both the people of the place itself and its existing and future target markets to see the place in a new and more productive way, and to lure them away from the "comfort zone" of their current perceptions towards something a little unfamiliar and a little more ambitious.

In my opinion, a good CI strategy should be able to do this, and in order to do so it needs to be six things, as explained below:

1 **Creative** (*surprising, arresting, memorable*)
   Creative is the opposite of boring: this is the factor which perhaps more than any other ensures that the nation, region or city stands a chance of being noticed in an increasingly noisy and crowded global marketplace.

   However, this imperative must be equated with the fact that the CI strategy for the country cannot be invented, so the creativity lies in the "take" or perspective that is given to the observation about the nation or the people; the acuteness of the observation, or its relationship to the "marketplace".

2 **Ownable** (*uniquely and unarguably about the place and not anywhere else*)

Ownability is a combination of truthfulness, credibility and distinct-iveness: is it true; is it something that people are prepared to accept as true; and does it effectively characterize one or more of the factors that objectively distinguish the place from its competitors?

The desired Competitive Identity of the country, city or region needs to be in some credible way connected to its current reputa-tion, or else the task becomes unfeasible. This must be informed by what the government of the place knows of its audience's per-ceptions of the place, rather than what they themselves believe about the place, because clearly the link has to be made by the audi-ence, not by the government.

3 **Sharp** *(highly focused, not generic, telling a very specific and definite story about the place, rather than a bland catch-all strategy)* There is often a slight air of inter-office memo language that per-vades the "visioneering" work of places, and this is usually because of the need for consensus among a wide group of stakeholders with different interests. What starts out as a fine intention to come up with the idea that everybody loves usually ends up as a desperate struggle to come up with the idea that nobody minds. Ideas that nobody minds are guaranteed to waste all money and all effort expended on them, for the simple reason that they will be of no inter-est to the target market. Unavoidably, strong ideas will polarize opin-ion and often do make people feel a little uncomfortable at first.

This quality of the strategy is as necessary as creativity to lift it above the ordinary, and to persuade the audience that this isn't sim-ply more of the same stuff they're hearing all the time. Lots of coun-tries, cities and regions are starting to work on their reputations, and many of them may have genuinely good plans and intentions, but somehow the initiative goes entirely unnoticed. This is often because their strategy just isn't daring or striking enough to make an indiffer-ent "customer" sit up and pay attention; it's all just a bit too general and slippery for people's imaginations to be able to get a good grip on it; in consequence, it might just start to change people's minds about the place if enough weight is put behind it, but it probably won't change their behaviour.

4 **Motivating** *(clearly points people towards new and different behaviours within government, the private sector and civil society that will lead to a changed image)*

A CI strategy can be good, true, ownable, believable, sharp, distinctive and creative, but still have no effect whatsoever: and this is usually because it's trying so hard to be good branding that it forgets to be good policy; it's a passive descriptor of the country's identity rather than an active force for sustaining or changing it. A CI strategy statement is not an advertising slogan. You will never see it on a billboard: it is a key for making people see themselves in a new way, and so behave in a new way, and so eventually be seen in a new way. The test for a viable CI strategy is the simple question, "Will it make us change the way we behave?"

5 **Relevant** *(a meaningful promise to the consumer)*
Good reputations work inside and outside: they are motivating to the population and stakeholders but must be equally so to customers or else they will not tie in well to the marketing function. Many strategies are too self-referential: they act as a reminder of the place's ethic and purpose rather than a promise to the "customer"; they offer no explicit relevance to his/her needs, and ultimately give no clear reason to "buy".

6 **Elemental** *(simple, usable, practical and robust enough to be meaningful to many people in many situations, over a very long period, and to be practically implementable within the context of each stakeholder's day-to-day business and private objectives)*
If the CI strategy is too hard to explain or too specific to a particular situation then it can't function as the single driving force for an entire country or region. Of course the problem with elemental things is that there aren't very many of them and they are usually a bit dull: the challenge is to discover a proposition that is as distinctive, creative, sharp and motivational as if it were a complex and sophisticated argument, but as robust, truthful, simple, universal and universally applicable as a basic element.

Years ago, when I ran an advertising firm, I discovered that the most valuable ideas *weren't* usually the ones that most people more or less liked. The really exciting ideas tended to polarize the group (some people absolutely loved them and some absolutely hated them), and we had often rejected these ideas because of the vehemence of certain team members' veto.

We probably wasted a lot of good ideas. Eventually, what I found to be much more important was the *strength of the reaction*, rather than the *level of acceptance* of the idea. The best thing for me to do was leave the room altogether and not come back in until the noise level had reached a certain pitch (the clapometer principle, if you will); then, when I came back in and found that half my team were standing on their chairs saying they'd rather sell their grandmothers than run with this idea, and the other half were standing on the table swearing they'd rather slash their own wrists than *not* run with this idea, I knew we were on to something interesting.

Why? Because it's far easier to turn a strong negative into a strong positive than it is to turn nothing into anything at all. And creative ideas – just like anything else whose purpose is to change people's minds about something – have to be strong stuff or they just won't register.

There is no doubt that making places – and especially smaller and poorer places – competitive in the global marketplace is a huge challenge today. A modestly enhanced and better-managed version of their current reputation might be of some help to some places, but it won't help a failing reputation reverse its decline, or help a poor place sell more products in rich markets, attract major investors, or greatly increase its inbound tourism figures. In coarse commercial terms, places must aim to become *megabrands* if they want to maximize the Competitive Identity effect: far more than places that are simply known to be attractive, they must try to become world-famous.

And what makes a megabrand – one of those brands that seem to do far more than just sell, but which inspire great loyalty, positive prejudice and lifelong interest? It's certainly not because they are advertised so much. As I have often said, a megabrand is one that finds itself, by accident or by design, in the path of major social change.

Countries, cities and regions need to aim to achieve the same effect. The purpose of the CI strategy must be to ensure that the country has what people want and need at the moment when large numbers of people discover what it is they want and need. They must anticipate where the next major social change is going to be, and make sure that the country is correctly positioned in the path of that change, and in a way that provides for the possibility of success into the foreseeable future. It goes without saying that the "product" itself must also be able to deliver on that promise, so the social changes observed must have some innate relevance to the country's resources, abilities or talents.

All Competitive Identity strategies must, as I have said, take their point of departure from the ways in which the country is presently perceived by the country's various overseas audiences and markets.

Often there is a temptation to discard these, because they are too familiar, out of date, and even insulting to the population of the country. But this temptation should be resisted, because the existing perception is what gives a country permission to start a dialogue with people in other places; whether it's Scotland's images of kilts, bagpipes and whisky, or Canada's moose, mountains and Mounties, it is essential to let people come through the door they know.

Among policy makers, it is a more common complaint that "people know about us for the wrong reasons" than "people know nothing about us". A place about which people know literally nothing, and have no prejudices or notions whatsoever, is literally a new product launch, a blank slate. However few places in reality are in this condition: most are associated with a single, simple, perhaps unhelpful or even negative cliché, and policy makers are understandably anxious to dispel the unhelpful cliché before going on to build positive brand equity in the mind of the consumer.

However, it is far easier, and more advisable, to take existing perceptions, however negative or inaccurate they might be, and attempt to build on these, gradually leading public perceptions in a new direction, than to break down the perceptions and start again. It is a principle of martial arts that, if a much heavier opponent is charging towards you, the last thing you should do is stand in his way and try to stop him, as you will be flattened. Far better to harness his forward momentum and help him to go somewhere that suits you rather than him: you stick out your foot, trip him up, and he will run on and crack his head against the wall.

I would always caution countries and their stakeholders against failing to conform at least to some degree to the reputation they already have, unless it is absolutely negative. Many a company has found itself losing a primary brand equity because it fell into the trap of believing that it "owned" the area: Volvo, for example, came to believe during the 1990s that it "owned" the concept of safety, and for a year stopped creating designs and running communications that stressed the safety of its cars. Within a year, Renault was identified by consumers in Europe as the safest car on the road.

It's a basic tenet of marketing that you never own a particular brand equity: you merely rent it, and must continue to pay the rent at regular intervals if you don't want to lose it. In exactly the same way, there are plenty of other countries that are frantic to stake a claim on heritage, culture, scenery, and so forth, and some of them have "product" in these areas which is equal to Scotland's or Canada's. If Scotland or Canada fail to pay the rent on these qualities, they might find that people forget them in a surprisingly short time.

There's an old concept from marketing strategy called the *Evoked Set* which is worth bearing in mind here. According to the theory, all purchasing decisions – in fact, all acts of selection – are made from a mental "shortlist" which never contains more than seven options. There is evidence from psychological research to show that this is a common pattern in all human decision-making. It seems that human beings can't cope with choosing between any more than this. So if a product isn't in the top seven, it simply will not be chosen; and it can't be added to the top seven because the list can never be extended. There is no number eight.

According to this analysis, if a country wants to attract more investors, tourists, talented immigrants, allies, consumers, trading partners or anyone else, it has to be on their shortlist. And to get on their shortlist, it needs to replace one of the seven countries that's already there. This obviously has important consequences for national strategy in all of these sectors: it's not about becoming more attractive in an abstract sense; it's about which other country you are going to take out first.

The structures of power

Whatever structures one adopts for managing a country's Competitive Identity, the translation of brand management from private to public sector practice will always be a political, intellectual and ethical challenge. The fact is that brand theory comes from commerce, and companies are very different organizations from countries; a contract of employment is a very different thing from a social contract; and the primary requirement of a company is to create profit, while the primary requirement of governance is to create viable communities.

After all, if you're branding a can of beans you don't need to ask the beans before you decide what to put on the label, but countries are different: they are made of people. If the process isn't fully democratic, fully transparent and fully inclusive, it will fail.

In the commercial sector, it is openly acknowledged that a certain heavy-handedness on the part of managers is usually required in order to achieve the kind of ruthless adherence to strategy and "on-message behaviour" which companies need. There is, in fact, little that is democratic in the way that most companies are run, and powerful brands are often the result of a very single-minded, even mildly deranged, "visionary" Chief Executive Officer who simply eliminates anybody who dares to deviate from the company line. To a degree, this is comprehensible: so much of the success of any branding venture is attributable to the amount of consistency which the company manages to achieve in its internal and external communications that a somewhat despotic management style is often found to be the simplest way to achieve this. In a company, it is also permissible to some degree, since one supposes that the employees are there of their own free will, and are being paid to perform in a way which the management decides is in the best interest of the company.

Countries, obviously, are different. A manager in a company may be ruthlessly single-minded and this can benefit the company enormously; the same approach by the leader of a country is called tyranny and seldom achieves positive results.

None the less, one knows from experience that getting many independent people and organizations, all with very different interests, opinions and agendas, to speak with a single voice is a hard thing to achieve through consensus. It's no accident that the cities and countries that have succeeded in building powerful and consistent new brands in a very short space of time are, more often than not, the ones that are run more like corporations than countries; Dubai and Singapore, to name but two, have both been famous for being run by a "Chief Executive" with a strong vision, and both have been extremely successful in building themselves a global brand.

For the majority of countries that are run in a more consensual fashion, however, one thing is clear: unless the government can find a way of achieving in its committees the same single-minded sense of purpose and control that the crazy brand visionary achieves within a privately-owned company, nothing will come of the Competitive Identity project, and it is doomed to fail.

Patience and unanimity of purpose are fundamental to changing the reputation of a country, but most countries face two obstacles to achieving these conditions: a lack of patience stemming from the four-year event horizon of most elected politicians (and a perfectly understandable desire to show measurable results within the electoral term); and the political difficulty of imposing shared purpose on the stakeholders of the national reputation, many of whom are commercial and political competitors, and over whom only the head of government or the head of state can exercise direct authority.

When one is dealing with a city or a small country, this problem is more tractable (and differences amongst stakeholder interests also tend to diminish in proportion to the gravity of the country's image problems), but in larger, more prosperous countries – and especially in regions composed of several countries – imposing a common strategy is politically impossible.

In reality, imposing a strategy by authority, even where sufficient authority exists, is unlikely to be a very effective approach. One can compel people to do most things, but one cannot compel them to be enthusiastic; and an enthusiastic population or workforce is a prerequisite for building a powerful international reputation. This is perhaps part of the reason why the very clear and powerful image strategies of some tyrants and dictators seldom achieve much impact beyond the borders of the state: the project can only succeed by compulsion, and exerts little relevance or magnetism in the "open marketplace".

The kind of shared vision and common purpose which is a precondition of successful Competitive Identity can only be achieved through "soft power", and by a critical mass of stakeholders voluntarily endorsing and agreeing to support the national or regional CI strategy. This fact places enormous demands on the creative abilities of the team that devises the strategy (it must be clear, inspiring and motivating enough for competing stakeholders to forget their differences temporarily and agree to "trade up" to it from their own convictions about what the strategy should be); on their salesmanship and rhetoric (it must be marketed internally); and on their willingness and ability to consult well and widely enough to build a sense of shared ownership of the idea without this hampering their ability to create something beyond mere political compromise.

The other problem – of political short-termism – is equally tricky to resolve. Countries with reigning monarchs have a distinct advantage here, in that royal families tend quite naturally to take a much longer view of the country's prospects than elected politicians do. For a member of a royal family, the country is the "family business", and it may be relatively unimportant to any particular monarch whether progress in the reputation of his or her country takes place during his or her lifetime or in those of his or her descendants. This almost oriental view of time is precisely what Competitive Identity requires if it is to achieve its best and most durable effects.

In Britain and many other Western monarchies, we tend to consider our royal families as being merely one of a range of tourism "products" which may or may not contribute to the country's heritage. This approach undeniably recognizes some of the "brand equity" inherent in royalty, but it may not be sustainable practice in the longer term. It is a primary tenet of a good brand strategy that one should contribute new equity to the brand as fast, or faster, than one exploits it. Just like sustainable forestry, good brand management recognizes that the goodwill inherent in any brand is a commodity in finite supply, and must be stored up against future need. Simply exploiting the brand equity of the royal family as a tourist attraction is spending that equity without replenishing it.

If, on the other hand, one considers a royal family as naturally committed, long-term guardians of the national reputation (which, one could argue, is one of the things that the more enlightened royal families always have been, notwithstanding changes in the vocabulary used), an interesting role for royalty in the modern world begins to suggest itself.

The looser the command structure, the softer the power has to be, and the best examples of places where hard power would be ineffectual even if it were possible to exert it are in regions such as the European Union where, quite literally, nobody is in charge, and no one individual or government has the power to impose a brand strategy on the population.

In such cases, rather than a top-down authoritarian structure, the best model for implementing a regional brand is probably something closer to Al-Qaeda than Josef Stalin: a loose network of semi-independent groups, each planning and carrying out its own activities and communications which are inspired by a commonly held belief in some simple, powerful mission.

The reference to terrorist networks may be in dubious taste, but there is no denying the strength, resilience and effectiveness of such a model. "Distributed leadership" – or self-organization – is exactly what brands need in complex organizations such as countries, and especially in regions.

Communicating the Competitive Identity strategy

When the time comes to start communicating the CI strategy to the stakeholders and ultimately to the general population of the country, city or region, the most common error is applying insufficient energy, vigour, imagination and commitment to this most critical part of the project.

Lots of governments in this situation tend to behave like guilty parents who don't spend enough time with their children: they buy them expensive presents instead such as glossy "brand books" and other materials which, as often as not, end up just gathering dust on people's shelves. But in order to achieve the right effect, face-to-face contact is indispensable. Documents (and even expensive multimedia presentations or glossy pamphlets) may provide valuable support, but simply can't achieve it on their own: anything which needs to be taken down from a shelf and consulted, or opened on a computer, is highly unlikely to change anybody's mind or behaviour.

There is no substitute for hand-picking a small team of champions, thoroughly imbued with the strategy and the task, and selected primarily for their ability to communicate a real passion for the subject, and sending them out on a mission to infect others with their enthusiasm, so that these can, in their turn, go on and teach others, and so on until the strategy becomes intrinsic to the entire region.

This part of the process works, in fact, very much like teaching. Years ago, I worked for a short time as a teacher, and made the same mistake which I imagine many beginners in that profession make: I started out with the assumption that teaching was all about me possessing a certain body of data which my students needed to share, and finding ways of passing that data on to them. I soon realized that this isn't the point at all: the quantity of information that students need to acquire after primary education is simply too great for it to be handed over, piece by piece, from teacher to pupil, and in any case, it is enormously hard to digest information given in this way.

In reality, there is no such thing as teaching, only learning, and making people hungry to learn. Real teaching is about having a passion for your subject, and knowing how to make that passion contagious.

And this fact is as true for communicating strategy amongst a large group of government and private sector stakeholders around a country as it is for teaching Shakespeare to teenagers. Give them the raw data, and they will discard it the moment your back is turned. But explain *why* it's there, *how* it got there, *why* it's important, *why* you love it, and *what* they can do with it, and you'll generate a hunger for acquiring more and more of that data which will last them for the rest of their lives.

CHAPTER 5

Implementing Competitive Identity

In the previous chapters, I have made it clear that advertising, graphic design and other forms of promotion are only able to offer a sensible return on investment when a well-defined product is being sold to a well-defined target audience. The most common examples of this are tourism, investment opportunities, cultural activities, and of course exports.

I have also stressed that these promotions should be coordinated with a national Competitive Identity strategy so that, instead of fighting against each other, each is helping to tell the same "story of the country", and also so that they are of uniformly high quality. In some cases, paid-for campaigns in the media, as well as graphic identity programmes, can be useful in helping to build that all-important sense of common purpose amongst the general population and in the corporate sector: in other words, for *internal* communications. But for addressing the image of the nation or city itself, these are simply the wrong tools for the task, and are most likely to be interpreted as empty propaganda by outsiders.

So when a country needs to do more than just sell its products, and wants to shift a negative, simplistic, outdated or misleading image – or, indeed, when it finds that selling those products is too difficult precisely because of that image – what are the right tools?

They are, as I hope has now become clear, the six points of the hexagon.

It was once common to speak of the "ship of state", but to illustrate how the points of the hexagon are used to achieve Competitive Identity, the best image I can find is of the nation (or the city or region) as a *spaceship* of state. The way to move that ship forwards is with finely calibrated thrusts of innovation and communication from the nation's six rockets: the tourist board and the companies, resorts and organizations in its sector; the cultural institute and the companies and organizations, events and initiatives, the sporting bodies, and other players in culture and heritage; the business and industrial sector and its products, services and companies; the government itself, its policies and investments, its missions abroad and public diplomacy initiatives; the people, their education, activities, their movements in and out of the country, the diaspora, the famous people and the general population; the investment, trade and education promotion agencies and their related locations, companies, public and private institutions, agencies and intermediaries.

The task of the team entrusted with coordinating and managing the CI strategy is to identify precisely the current position of the "spaceship"; to identify a viable and useful destination; to create the necessary team spirit so that a working majority of the stakeholders and the general population understands, supports and believes in the mission; to ensure that those six "thrusters" are all in place, working properly and efficiently, fuelled with the necessary funding, and are fully synchronized and not pushing against each other; and to steer a straight course to the destination.

Tourism and Competitive Identity

Tourism is in most cases the most important and most powerful of the nation's six "booster rockets", for the simple reason that it has permission to brand the country directly. Publics are generally dismissive of direct communications from national governments or their agencies, and – not surprisingly, since they are never selling a specific product to a specific audience – are unsure how to react to them. Communications from tourist boards, on the other hand, are seen as a legitimate representation of the country to the global audience. The fact that the product on offer is, explicitly or implicitly, a holiday in the country, is of secondary importance: what counts is that the messages are able to give people new information, and most importantly new images, about the country. They can tell people what the place looks like, what sort of people live there, what sort of things those people do and make, the climate, the food, the culture and the history of the country.

Even if the destination is too expensive, too inaccessible, too small or too environmentally sensitive to accept large numbers of visitors, the channel of tourism marketing can be a valuable way to broadcast the country's image and reputation for foreign audiences: a kind of "vicarious visit". These audiences may, as a result of their favourable impression of the place, be more inclined to buy products from the country that carry some of its magic, consume services that are delivered by the people who have been so favourably presented in the tourism promotion, be interested in the cultural productions of the country, and to recommend it to others, who perhaps will visit the country in person one day. Both New Zealand and Australia have used tourism promotion in this way to communicate an idea of the country that has more to do with building a "global brand" for the country than with persuading large numbers of people to visit (although both countries have succeeded in increasing the numbers of visitors as well).

There's an analogy for this approach in public service advertising. In most countries, it is not possible for the police force to use paid media to communicate directly with the public, so they find it difficult to present a complete picture of their aims and values to the general population. Most of them, however, discovered long ago that by careful wording of their recruitment advertising (which of course they are allowed to do), clearly communicating the kind of people they are and the kind of values they espouse through careful descriptions of the kind of people they want to hire, and by carefully placing it prominently in the general media (which, of course, nobody can stop them from doing) they are able to add at least one strand of entirely controlled communication about themselves directly to the public, rather than relying totally on second-hand communications through the medium of editorial.

Effective tourism promotion can also affect many other choices, including major investment decisions. Most of us find it difficult to think of things in an entirely abstract way, and tend to attach visual images to our thoughts: were it possible to look inside the mind of a senior executive at the moment in which she or he is considering in which country to make a major investment, the chances are we would see a "snapshot" of how he or she imagines that the country looks. This mental postcard, if it hasn't been supplied by a personal visit, may well have been placed there by the country's tourist board: if the image is an attractive one, it may create positive bias towards that country. If, on the other hand, the tourism images are absent or of poor quality, the predominant images will more likely have been supplied by news media, literature, history lessons, other people's experiences, and a host of other less controllable and less predictable sources.

As I mentioned in Chapter 3, visiting a country also tends to improve people's attitudes towards the whole nation, its people and products, so tourism is also important because it encourages what in the private sector would be thought of as "product trial". Many countries are more pleasing in reality than in imagination, and there is often much truth in the frequently heard lament "If only people could just come here and see, they would change their minds about our country." Tourism does this, as well as selling holidays, and, of course, as the United Nations World Tourism Organization has developed numerous models to prove, generates enormous secondary benefits for the economy and the employment of a country.

However, creating strategic agreement between the tourist board and other stakeholders in the national reputation is not always an easy task. The image presented by the tourist industry may be seen as irrelevant, unhelpful or even damaging to the country's other international initiatives, especially promoting for trade or inward investment. Many countries enjoy a valuable tourist image based on wild, empty countryside, quaint old-world charm, and a populace perceived as warm-hearted, uncomplicated, old-fashioned, rustic and utterly unsophisticated: hardly a useful image to have lodged in the minds of multinational corporations deciding where to build their newest semiconductor plant.

Such contrasts and contradictions, for the very reason that they exist in the real world, can ultimately be resolved, harmonized and believably communicated in a country's CI programme. It takes creativity, objectivity, good brand management, and a deep understanding of the way that consumer logic works (or can be encouraged to work) in each target country and each target audience. Quite simply, countries are contradictory, and one has to deal with this.

If consistency can be achieved, however, the benefits are considerable. Such a strategy can save money rather than cost money: simply coordinating the messages that the country's different stakeholders are already sending out, and linking them all to a powerful and distinctive CI strategy, can result in a massive increase in salience without the need to make any increase in marketing spend.

Brands and Competitive Identity

Brands have a particular power to accelerate and lead changes in the public perceptions of countries: whether we like it or not, they are increasingly important vectors of national image and reputation, even of culture. While an older audience might associate Switzerland, for example, with William Tell (culture), cheese, chocolate, cuckoo-clocks and banking (unbranded produce and services), mountains and skiing (tourism), or neutrality (foreign policy), the first associations of younger people are far more likely to be Swatch or Swiss Army (branded products). Similarly, the first reaction of most children when asked what they know about Japan is "Sony", "Nintendo", "Hello Kitty", "Sailor Moon" or "Pokémon".

One commercial consequence of such brand-informed images is that they can stereotype countries in a two-dimensional way which makes it harder for exporters of "non-typical" products to gain acceptance in overseas markets. For example, Italy's brand image as a fashion and style producer made it very difficult for Olivetti, a computer manufacturer, to create a successful export business; German fashion brands, such as Hugo Boss and Jil Sander, have always downplayed their national origins because fashion products don't chime with the consumer perception of a rational and technical Germany which, as I mentioned earlier, is generated and sustained by brands including Bosch, Siemens, Porsche, AEG, BMW and Mercedes.

This is a relatively minor problem, however, and it's hardly beyond the wit of a competent marketing organization to get around it: the real risk is that this convenient shorthand gets in the way of a deeper understanding of a country's cultural output.

As brands gradually become the dominant channel of communication for national identity, it becomes ever more vital to push the other channels: by encouraging first-hand experience of the country via tourism, by the careful management of international perceptions of a nation's foreign policy decisions, and by the representation of national culture.

None the less, it is worth pointing out that products make far more effective ambassadors for the national image than promotional campaigns, because they make money rather than costing money; people welcome products and avoid advertisements; and people take products into their homes and keep them, rather than throwing them away or deleting them as soon as they can.

The difficulty often lies in persuading the owners of powerful commercial brands to acknowledge their country of origin in their marketing or packaging. It seems likely that if Nokia were to make more noise about being Finnish, it would benefit the image of Finland tremendously: but if you ask executives at Nokia why they don't do so, they will explain that companies need to localize their marketing in order to appeal to consumers, that Nokia is a global company with more non-Finnish than Finnish employees and more real estate outside than inside Finland, and so forth. The real reason, I suspect, is that they know perfectly well that Nokia is a bigger brand than Finland, and they fear that if the two were more closely attached to each other, the brand equity would all flow from the stronger to the weaker, and benefit the brand image of Finland at the expense of the brand image of Nokia.

This is a very common dilemma for countries attempting to leverage the power of their exporters. In reality, I suspect that Nokia and other brands from smaller markets that choose to appear "global" may be underestimating the power of their brands: it depends of course on the degree of attachment, but if consumers feel an attachment, a loyalty towards a particular brand, it seems unlikely that they would change their minds about the brand if they discovered one day that the brand originated in a surprising, small, poor, or exotic country: it seems more likely that they would change their minds about the country, and take it as an additional mark of distinction for the brand that it comes from somewhere rather original and unexpected; indeed, it would confer a certain prestige on the loyal consumer for having the style and originality to choose products that don't come from America, Japan or Germany.

The brands from bigger and richer countries which still feel nervous about "limiting" their brands by attaching them too strongly to their country of origin might consider that in a time when the products in the shops could come from almost anywhere, their country of origin, their rootedness, actually seems to become ever more important to the consumer.

The reason must surely be that people find it easier to like and trust *real* brands, not synthetic constructs without a history or a home. Many companies which, a decade ago, were rushing to create "global" brands are starting to see that however attractive a global brand might appear to the corporation and its shareholders, it's not something which consumers always care for.

As part of the process which leads to the vague nirvana of globalness, lots of companies have attempted systematically to remove every clue about their country of origin from their products and services. British Airways' fateful decision in 1997 to graduate from mere national carrier to global travel brand, drop the explicit reference to its country of origin and the Union flag, and carry images from many different nations on its tailplanes, was one of several instances of this type. But in their rush to appear global, BA overlooked the crucial point that a global brand isn't a brand which comes from nowhere: in many of the most successful cases, it is a brand which may be *sold* everywhere, but *comes* from somewhere quite definite. Coca-Cola, Pepsi, McDonald's, Nike, Levi's, Timberland and Marlboro, for example, are only global brands by grace of the fact that they are most decidedly from America.

British Airways would never have become the world's favourite airline if it hadn't been, first and foremost, *British* Airways: the age-old popular perception of "brand Britain" (methodical, punctual, predictable, efficient, traditional, heritage-obsessed, class-ridden, status-driven, ceremonious, perhaps a bit boring) makes Britain the ultimate, the supremely logical country of origin for any brand in the business of air travel, hospitality and tourism. It's easy to be wise after the event, but by cutting off its connection with its homebrand, British Airways simply pulled the plug on its principal brand equity.

In 2001 the airline's new chief executive, Rod Eddington, an Australian, ordered the Union Jacks to be painted back on the planes. It often takes the objective viewpoint of an outsider to understand the essence of a nation's image.

It's not so surprising that people want brands to come from somewhere. After all, the first time you meet someone, it's human nature to ask them where they're from: and as the likelihood of that person coming from the same place as you do becomes smaller with every year that passes, the question becomes increasingly relevant. A country of origin is *hard equity*, which in many cases doesn't need to be built from scratch because it already exists in the consumer's mind, and has a definite shape and form.

There's no doubt that consumers are increasingly asking brands where they come from, and the correct answer is *not* "wherever you want". Many companies might just find that whilst they're burbling on about "planet Earth" or "around the world", the consumer has gone away in search of something with a little more integrity.

Of course, if you ask them in the abstract, most people agree that coming from countries such as Germany, Italy, America or Japan adds credibility and appeal to products, while coming from a developing country – unless it's one of those rare exceptions, such as Brazil, which happen to have a natural storehouse of positive imagery – is more likely to reduce a product's appeal. The perception is that companies in such countries don't manufacture to the same standards as companies in the North: they use shoddy materials and cheap labour, and the end product is inherently less valuable. With such thoughts in the consumer's mind, charging a premium price for a brand that doesn't already have a loyal consumer base seems unthinkable.

These prejudices are hard to fight, even though they contradict what the majority of consumers in the West already know: that most of the products bearing their most valued brand names are actually manufactured – to the standards which such brand-owners require – in poor countries.

We are left with a vicious circle: it's hard to sell a branded product for a high price if it is known to come from a country not perceived to produce high quality products; yet the country will never earn that reputation unless its brand-owners start telling consumers where they come from.

In one way, the corporations which own so many of the biggest global brands have already started the process of breaking this perceptual cycle, and certainly without meaning to, simply by acknowledging where they source their products. Over the last few decades, consumers have become very familiar with those humble little stickers on the underside of their American or European-branded toys and running shoes and domestic appliances ("Made in China", "Made in Vietnam", "Made in Thailand", "Made in Mexico"), and they have quietly absorbed the fact that a great many of the products they buy are manufactured (to the high standards required by those American and European brand-owners, naturally) in poorer countries. As we have seen, it doesn't much affect their beliefs about the basic "nationality" of the brand, but it is noticed, and remembered, as a separate fact.

The American and European brand-owners could hardly have done their supplier nations a better favour. This low-pressure public relations campaign on behalf of the emerging world has effectively communicated to hundreds of millions of consumers – with far more patience and subtlety than most global companies ever apply to the promotion of their own brands – the simple fact that most of the best products in the world are now manufactured in developing countries, thus neatly paving the way for manufacturers in those countries to start developing their own brands, and for people in the First World to buy them.

The perception only has to be enhanced a little further, and brought more explicitly to the consumer's attention, and another barrier preventing the development of global brands from emerging markets will have been removed.

Using "country of origin" more creatively

It's clear that a home country with strong, positive and universally-recognized associations of trust, quality and integrity is a major advantage to its manufacturers as they face the harsh realities of global competition. In this respect, it's just like the way a new product from a well-known company is accepted by loyal consumers: the "parent brand" stands in as a proxy for personal experience of the product, and encourages trial in a way which a new product from an unknown company can almost never do.

For a brand's home country to add this helpful dose of free additional equity, the product should "chime" with its country of origin in the consumer's mind, and some kind of logic must link the two.

This logic may be simple or creative: in the case of manufactured brands, it could be the straightforward logic of category expertise which (for example) links Benckiser, a manufacturer of household cleaning products, with a new household cleaning product; or it could be the more lateral sort of logic that links Caterpillar, a manufacturer of bulldozers, with rugged footwear. In exactly the same way, brands from countries can range from simple national produce – pizza from Italy or soft drinks from America – to more unexpected but equally attractive pairings, such as skis from Slovenia, clothing from Australia, or phones from Finland.

When you try to match provenance with product, there are some pairings that clearly make brand sense, and others that just don't. People might well buy Indian accountancy software or even a stylish Lithuanian raincoat, and although I'm tempted to say that they probably wouldn't buy Peruvian modems or Croatian perfume, attitudes can and do change quickly. Fifteen years ago, who would have believed that Europeans could be happily consuming Tsingtao beer and Lenovo computers from China or Proton cars from Malaysia?

Only one thing is certain about the strange phenomenon that marketers reassuringly call "consumer behaviour": predictions are more often wrong than right, and many great marketing successes have occurred as a consequence of an inspired or obstinate marketer choosing to ignore what consumer research identified as "what consumers want".

As any experienced researcher knows, research often tells us little more than what consumers have seen before, and what they find reassuring. The simple fact is that we often don't *know* what we want until we see it for the first time, and part of the skill of the marketer is thinking of things that are unlike anything we have seen before. Research is an essential part of learning about the market, helping to understand consumer needs and testing new approaches, but it is never a substitute for creativity, and is the worst possible tool for creating new products or services. The last person who can tell you what's the next big thing is the person who is actually going to buy it when it comes along.

When a country does have the courage, insight and creativity to move away from the classic paradigm of "national produce" and celebrate the fact that it produces brands that make you think again about the country which produces them, the results can be far more noticeable, and consequently far more profitable. Somewhere in the mysterious processes of consumer logic (or perhaps "logic" really isn't the right word for it), Caterpillar boots and Slovenian skis made sense, and the resulting brand extension benefits both the company's core business and the new business: it really is a case of two and two making five.

Culture and Competitive Identity

The role of culture in promoting a country is often thought of as problematic: governments acknowledge that there is clearly some kind of requirement to represent the cultural attainments of a country, but there is a concern that they don't "sell" – or provide return on investment – in the same way that inward investment, exports or tourism do. So culture becomes relegated to the status of a "not for profit" activity, a kind of charitable or philanthropic obligation.

However, to see representing culture as an obligation is to misunderstand its power to communicate a country's true spirit and essence. In truth, culture plays an essential role in the process of enriching a country's reputation, in driving public perceptions towards a fuller and more durable understanding of the country and its values.

Culture uniquely provides this extra dimension because, in the face of the consumer's suspicion of commercial messages, culture is self-evidently "not for sale": to use a cynical metaphor, it's a "promotional gift" that comes with the commercial identity. Culture is, if you like, the rich harmonic accompaniment to the simple, accessible, easily memorable melody of commercial competitive advantage. You can whistle a country's commercial brand, and not its cultural counterpoint; but the former is worth very much less without the latter.

Another of the values of culture in Competitive Identity is that each culture, like its geography, is a truly unique feature of its country. Once you start looking at features and benefits, in classic marketing style, you are inevitably driven into common and non-unique territory, and one country starts to resemble another. A typical example of this trap is the tourism campaign which, by selling the feature of blue sea and sky with sandy beaches and the user benefit of relaxation and a golden tan, makes all seaside destinations indistinguishable from each other.

Representation of a country's culture provides the country's image with that all-important quality of dignity which, arguably, commercial brands can do without, but countries cannot. The Western consumer's knowledge of Japanese art, poetry, cuisine and philosophy, for example, however shallow it might be, functions as an important counterpoint to the commercial image of Japan: productivity, miniaturization, technology, and so on. It helps to reduce the potentially threatening image of a highly, even aggressively efficient, producer nation by reassuring consumers that they are buying goods manufactured by real human beings, not automata. And Japanese pop culture provides the counterpart to the rather joyless perception that might otherwise prevail, while also feeding imagery – and hence added attraction – directly into exported products. This process is common to almost all representations of pop culture, which are by definition closely linked to the commercial aspects of national promotion.

In a similar way, perceptions of Germany as the home of great classical music, literature and philosophy ought to help provide an extra human dimension to the sterile, brand-generated and ultimately copiable image of Germany as a mere factory producing expensive, highly functional and rather overengineered consumer products. The fact that, at least according to my research, these elements are very much underrepresented in the national image means that the reputation of Germany is really only firing on one cylinder.

Italy is blessed with a better natural balance in its reputation: if Italy's image was only communicated through its commercial brands, which are mainly in the food, fashion and lifestyle arena, it might seem like a shallow, superficial, fun-loving and highly stylish place but without much depth; so the high awareness of figures including Michelangelo, Dante, Leonardo, Galileo, Vivaldi and Verdi (not to mention Luciano Pavarotti, Roberto Benigni and Andrea Bocelli in more recent times and in a more populist vein), as well as the "sub-brands" of Venice, Florence and Rome, provide a profound counterpoint to a very attractive melody.

The challenge for all countries is to find ways of continually presenting and re-presenting their past cultural achievements alongside their modern equivalents in ways that are fresh, relevant and appealing to younger audiences. This task is made ever more complex by the increasing plurality of modern societies: to celebrate the glories of a typically somewhat monocultural past without marginalizing or seeming to ignore the multiracial reality of the country's modern day population is a real quandary for most countries. Still, since the only solution is to give equal emphasis to present-day cultural enterprise, it is basically a productive dilemma, because it lessens the temptation for countries to rest on their laurels and live in the past.

Race is very important, and is, in fact, one of the main reasons why so many countries – and richer European countries in particular – need to start thinking very hard about how well their traditional international image reflects their present reality, even though that image might appear to be in very good shape. Perhaps this is one part of the explanation for France's current racial tensions: the "brand story" of France, the way the country is viewed, and to some extent the way it still represents itself to the outside world, is still an old story of a white Christian European power. But many French people who are neither white nor Christian feel that the national story leaves them out: and of course that causes bitter resentment.

Many countries now need to reassess the way they identify themselves and communicate that identity to the world in the light of their changing populations. It's one of the biggest tasks facing governments today, and is an acute challenge for the way in which Competitive Identity is developed.

In the mind of the consumer, culture also works in many different ways as a metaphor for personality, and people deduce a great deal about the inner qualities of a nation through its cultural enterprises. Sport equals strength, courage, physical prowess, agility, determination, team spirit, honour, fair play, and so on. Pop music equals street credibility, flexibility, creativity, imagination, a sense of fun.

The cultural aspect of national image is irreplaceable and uncopiable because it is uniquely linked to the country itself; it is reassuring because it links the country's past with its present; it is enriching because it deals with non-commercial activities; and it is dignifying because it shows the spiritual and intellectual qualities of the country's people and institutions.

Culture is a more eloquent communicator of national image than commercial brands, even if it does work more slowly. Brands in any case will always have their own commercial imperatives, and will, quite rightly, only comply with the official country branding strategy as long as it helps their sales. By contrast, the communication of culture can be pretty much agenda-free, as it is mercifully not answerable to the tyranny of return on investment, and its stakeholders usually ask for nothing more onerous than fair and truthful representation.

Case notes: America and the power of culture

America's cultural output, by contrast, has been a highly marketable commodity since the late nineteenth century. It has always paid its own way, and what's more has always been seen by American governments as one of the "hard" techniques for building the national reputation.

The US government had led cultural projects abroad since at least 1938, when the Department of State's Division of Cultural Relations was established, and the Office of the Coordinator of Inter-American Affairs (established in 1941) supported exhibitions and other artistic events in Latin America. But it was in fighting the Cold War that the federal government made a priority of showcasing American art abroad. Soviet propaganda relentlessly portrayed the US as a cultural wasteland, and with some success, so America felt it was vital to respond to this untruth in the strongest of terms.

One reason why culture works so well in building Competitive Identity for countries is that consumers aren't as suspicious of it as they are of commercial messages. Even if it's popular culture, it's still art, or at least entertainment, so people relax their vigilance, and don't look for hidden agendas. At least until recently, Hollywood movies could get away with some fairly explicit celebration of American values, and foreign audiences just sat back and enjoyed the show.

And cinema, music, art and literature are important because they add colour, detail and richness to people's perception of the country, and help them to get to know the place almost as well as if they'd been there; better, in fact, because the picture that's painted is often a little idealized, and all the more magical for being intangible and incomplete.

Some of those great American commercial brands have done a marvellous job in sketching the outlines of Brand America: wealth, independence, ruggedness, dependability, individualism, youthfulness, fun, and so on. But American films, music, literature and art have filled in the details, and built Brand America into a rich and satisfying thing for hundreds of millions of people around the world to encounter, to explore, to get to know and trust over many years.

As a result, no other country has ever penetrated so deeply into the lives and imaginations of so many people around the world. Almost everyone who came into contact with books, radio, television, music, cinema, video games or branded products during the twentieth century has been touched by America, and large numbers of them grew to love it with a passion.

Every little boy, from Hong Kong to Paraguay or Iceland to South Africa, who longed for a cowboy hat, a sheriff's star and a brace of pistols, and every little girl who longed for Barbie dolls, was dreaming of America. Little wonder that when they became teenagers, they reached first for the American records, happily paid a bit more for American cigarettes, drank the Real Thing and, later still, found it felt absolutely right working for an American firm, and taking the family on holiday to Florida.

Consider the intense and lifelong loyalty of *billions* of such people, and you begin to have a picture of the power and extent of Brand America, and of the critical importance of culture as a building-block of that brand.

Making culture magnetic

Culture can often play a critical role in moving the current image of a country towards a more useful one. Culture is the component that is absolutely necessary in order to make the image of any place properly satisfying, especially in the case of countries which, as I mentioned earlier, suffer from an image that is largely or exclusively based on tourism.

Culture it is next-door to tourism (indeed, cultural tourism is often identified as the highest-yielding and fastest-growing area of tourism), and it is the area that can start to make a connection between people's interest in the place itself and their interest in the life of the place. A rich cultural life makes a complete place rather than just a tourist destination, a place worth visiting at different times of the year, a place with a broader social appeal but particularly to the higher-end, higher-yielding, somewhat older and usually well-behaved visitors that most tourist destinations need above all others.

Most moderately developed countries and regions have a range of cultural attractions to offer the visitor in the form of historical and heritage sights; relatively few have attractions that really create a sense of the *cultural life* of the place. Yet new attractions and events of the right sort are ideal for putting a new lens in front of the country and starting to change people's minds about the kind of place it really is.

Rather than the sort of cultural event that the right kind of person already visiting the country might want to include in their itinerary, what places really need are the kinds of event that will give people a reason to go to the country in the first place. Creativity is what makes the difference between enjoyable events that play a role in enhancing the place, and events that create their own market, events that are magnetic and make the place a destination in its own right.

Yet the raw materials for a rich, varied and attractive cultural life are often lying around, just waiting to be assembled in a new way. What places need are the people with the imagination, the ambition, the creativity and the energy to make these connections, give them life, and make extraordinary things happen; they need the encouragement and the moral and financial support to help them to think creatively and act on their creative ideas; in short, the country needs to build a spirit of creative entrepreneurship.

In order for an event or attraction to become a magnet in its own right, it either has to have *mature pulling power*, built up through many years of excellence (for example, the Montreux Jazz Festival, the Burning Man festival in Nevada or the Oberammergau Passion Play), or be so unique and irresistible that its pulling power is intrinsic and *born great*, and needs only a very short time to become established (such as Cirque du Soleil, London's Tate Modern or the Live8 concerts).

Most of the attractions that appear to be born great are actually helped along by substantial funding, and there's no doubt that a Burj al-Arab, an Eden Project or a Guggenheim Museum can really put an unknown place on the map.

Fortunately, money isn't the only thing that can achieve this effect. There are also places and events that manage to pull off the same trick without huge investments in infrastructure or marketing: they are simply *magnetic ideas* that seize the imagination and are compelling by their very nature.

Three good examples of these are:

(a) the Ice Hotel in Sweden, which cost relatively little to create but became an almost overnight success and, according to the Nation Brands Index, is now the best-known tourist attraction in Sweden;

(b) the Pike Place Fish Market in Seattle, which was just a fish market for about a hundred years until one fishmonger decided to get his shop assistants to juggle with their fish: it's now the city's main attraction and draws tourists (and customers) from all over the USA;

(c) Isla Mujeres, a small island off the coast of Mexico which was close to destitution until they decided to paint every building on the island using a palette of authentic Mexican colours. The "Painting the Island" project gained an enormous amount of free global publicity: American cruise ships now regularly stop at the island, and the place has an economy.

What these attractions and others like them all have in common is the fact that they are themselves clear and powerful brands. Their fundamental attraction can be described in a few simple words, and this is in the nature of all good brands: they give people a great story to tell each other. Building a brand (and this is equally true of branding attractions and branding nations) isn't done by selling directly to the entire marketplace: that's just not feasible. It's done by devising or discovering a proposition that is inherently so original, irresistible and unforgettable that it is simply self-propelling. To set the ball rolling it's only necessary to persuade a few people to try it, like it, and help and encourage them to talk persuasively about it to the much larger number of people *they* know, and so on.

Marketing experts like to talk about viral marketing, buzz marketing, word of mouth, peer influence and cascade marketing as if they were somehow different from classic marketing, but in fact all good marketing is viral, and always has been. People are the only efficient and cost-effective advertising medium for reaching large numbers of other people. The brand has to be like a little travelling-salesman kit that is given to the limited audience one actually *can* afford to reach, and which equips *them* to spread the word on behalf of the brand to millions of other people. And they will do this for free, rather effectively, time and time again, simply because they *want* to, and because somebody has succeeded in firing their imagination.

"How far would I go just to see that?" is a good measure of the magnetism of an idea, and a crucial test-question for any new event or attraction that is being proposed. Unless it produces and impeccably executes two one-hundred-mile ideas for every twenty-mile idea, the region or country is unlikely to change its image.

Culture includes sport: Hong Kong has achieved a lot of reputational capital from the revival of its famous Dragon Boat Races, and there's no reason why any other country or region shouldn't revive or invent some unique indigenous sports which reflect some attribute of the place and the life of the people around it.

The key point is that not having dozens of world-class events or attractions doesn't mean that a place is doomed to fare less well than the places that do: one can *build* heritage, *invent* attractions, *make* a place magnetic. And there's nothing at all shameful or dishonest about inventing heritage (as long as one doesn't make false claims about its origins, of course): after all, even old things were new once, and part of the art of being a good ancestor is starting lots of valuable traditions in one's own lifetime so that one's descendants can benefit from them later.

Making magnetic attractions is often a matter of taking a basic cliché that everyone knows about the place as the starting point (for instance, Sweden is cold, Mexico is colourful, Seattle is a lively fishing port, Hong Kong is on the water and Chinese culture is full of dragons). Then one uses the human and natural capital that's lying around and sculpts it together to make a magnet. And of course there's nothing that says every idea has to be on a huge scale: even a tiny, perfect idea such as a new way of selling fish can play its part in building the fame of the city, region or country. Not every idea can be a hundred-mile or a thousand-mile idea, but even a ten-mile or twenty-mile idea helps promote the place: the important thing is that they are all aligned, all pointing the same way, all telling the same story about the place.

The Pike Place Fish Market in Seattle is a good example of the kind of simple innovation that can completely galvanize an ordinary business and turn it into a hundred-mile magnet (in the case of Pike Place it's actually a three-thousand-mile magnet, because people come from across the country just to see it). There's a particular kind of attitude that's necessary in order to achieve this sort of brand turnaround, and it's worth quoting an employee of Pike Place recounting a conversation he had with the founder just after they launched:

> We asked him: "How are we going to become world famous? We don't have any money to advertise!" Jim told us we didn't have to know how to become world famous. He told us that when you're generating a powerful vision, the future just unfolds. He told us not to believe in it. We just had to be it. He pointed out that there's a big difference between a belief about something and the actual thing itself. Muhammad Ali didn't say, "I believe I am the greatest." He said, "I am the greatest."[8]

That's the spirit that any wise government will be looking out for – and ultimately trying to breed – when building Competitive Identity.

The population and Competitive Identity

The term "public diplomacy" is closer in meaning to Competitive Identity if the word "public" is applied to the messenger as well as the audience: in other words, when a substantial part of the population is motivated and energized through a benign national ambition, and instinctively seizes every opportunity to tell the world about its country. If traditional diplomacy is government-to-government (G2G) and public diplomacy is government-to-people (G2P), then effective nation branding also includes an element of P2P. Some countries, such as Italy and America, seem to achieve the P2P spirit quite naturally, while others, such as Britain and Germany, find it much more of a problem.

When the entire population is galvanized into becoming the mouthpiece of a country's values and qualities, *then* you have an advertising medium that is actually equal to the enormous task of communicating something so complex to so many. We've all seen this approach in action, even if we've seldom seen it done consistently or thoroughly.

All of us, I think, have the experience of feeling special feelings about a particular country that we have never visited.

My special country was always Sri Lanka. Long before I went to Sri Lanka the place had a special attraction for me: when Sri Lanka appeared in the news, I paid it particular attention, I was always interested in going there on holiday and, on the rare occasions where I saw a product that was made in Sri Lanka, I somehow was more interested in that than the other products. For a long time I couldn't work out where this odd prejudice had come from, and then I remembered that years before, at a conference, I had met a man from Sri Lanka. We'd got talking about his country during a break in the conference, and he had been so passionate, sincere and so obviously in love with his own country that I was completely sold. From that moment, I thought that Sri Lanka must be heaven on earth. And years later, I went to Sri Lanka and had a rather miserable time, and I *still* went away thinking it was the best country in the world.

It occurred to me then that I had been subjected to the most powerful piece of marketing I had ever experienced in my life: it was 100 per cent effective, because it even survived a disappointing experience with the product. It was, as far as I can tell, 100 per cent permanent. It was, as far as Sri Lanka is concerned, 100 per cent free, because of course my Sri Lankan friend wasn't paid to go around telling people he met at conferences about how wonderful his native country was. And, unlike all other communication media, using the population to spread the word also gives you 100 per cent global coverage.

This, it seems to me, is the real power of P2P diplomacy. The ultimate aim towards which Competitive Identity should aspire is creating such a sense of pride and purpose that the entire population begins, almost by instinct, to perform such acts of conversion, every day of their lives: an impossible target to attain, of course, but the direction in which one should strive could not be clearer.

It's true that each individual "branding" action, and its effect on the whole world's perceptions of the country, may seem heartbreakingly tiny, hardly even worth doing: a mere drop in the ocean. But the ocean is made of drops, and what is truly heartbreaking is when thousands of people and companies and products and politicians and personalities and cultural artefacts are drop-drop-dropping messages every single day about their country and it doesn't amount to anything, because there's no method behind it, no guidance, no strategy, no vision, no common purpose.

Education and Competitive Identity

Education plays an important role in establishing the image of the country for future generations and building future visitors, residents, investors, advocates and supporters. If, for example, schoolchildren in one country are taught about the history or geography of another country, and if the teaching is successful, then the image and the existence of the place will be firmly established in their minds, quite possibly forever.

When children learn about a particular country in their geography lessons, it is clear that they quickly build up a special feeling about the place that is strong, personal and likely to result in a lifelong loyalty to a place they have never even visited. And one can see that, if the subject is well taught and the country winningly presented, it can create more pester-power marketing than years of deliberate efforts by places such as Disney World and Legoland to achieve precisely this effect. Children can remain more or less indifferent to endless television commercials specifically designed to brainwash them into forcing their parents to take them to such attractions, yet the impact of a piece of educational promotion by another country is often far greater and certainly more lasting. This clearly has something to do with respect for the messenger – children may well trust what a teacher tells them rather than what an advertisement on the television sells them – but it probably has just as much to do with the deeper impact of a proper learning process rather than pure one-way entertainment.

Education is also important in the reverse sense: over the coming generations, countries also need to start educating children to be better informed, more enthusiastic and prouder advocates of their own nation. A Competitive Identity is one of the few effective ways of controlling population loss: if teenagers and young adults sense that where they live is at the heart of things, admired and respected by people in other places around the world, a place they are proud to call their own because of the positive reaction they get from everybody they meet, they are far less likely to succumb to the brand power of somewhere more glamorous and further afield. Like so much that drives the psychology of young adults, it's a question of self-respect.

In a more practical way, it's good to work out ways of teaching children from a very young age how to be welcoming to strangers: any place that depends on outside visitors for its survival is failing in a basic duty of care if it doesn't provide this kind of training or sensitization for its young people. Later, the training can of course become even more practical and directly vocational, and much good work continues to be done in training for hospitality, conservation and leisure.

Sport and Competitive Identity

The City Brands Index reveals that the huge global awareness of the Olympic Games and its close association with the host cities is a significant factor for the reputations of those cities. Nowhere is this more evident than in the case of the 2000 Sydney Olympics, an event which produces an average international awareness of 87 per cent, dwarfing all other associations of any sort with any other city. In most of our country panels, the spontaneous association of Sydney with the Olympic Games is virtually 100 per cent. It is no exaggeration to say that the modern image of Sydney was built on the Opera House and the Olympic Games, and in consequence much of the high equity of Brand Australia (in 2005 the No. 1 country in Q2 of the Nation Brands Index).

The other remarkable factor about the salience given by the Olympics is how slowly it decays. A significant number of our panellists still spontaneously make associations between Paris and the Olympic Games, even though the last Games held there was in 1924. Even *future* host cities, such as Beijing and London, gain awareness purely through popular anticipation of the Olympics. As the chart below shows, there is a gradual decline in popular association between the Olympic Games and its host cities over a period of about 80–100 years but, as the still high awareness of the 1964 Tokyo Olympics shows (it was the first televised Olympics), the decline is by no means inevitable (see Figure 5.1).

Next to the Olympics, other sporting events pale into insignificance: the football World Cup (surely one of the biggest events after the Olympics)

Figure 5.1   Association of Olympic Games with host city

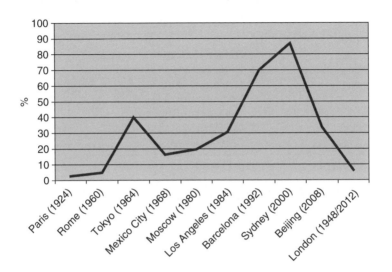

barely registers in the City Brands Index: the highest score is an average of 18 per cent for the 1998 World Cup in Paris. Obviously this low score is partly because the World Cup is hosted by a country rather than by a city, so the branding effect is more diffuse, and yet none of the American host cities of the previous World Cup in 1994 is still associated with the event by more than 1 per cent of our panellists.

The only other sporting events mentioned by substantial numbers of our panellists are the Tour de France, also associated with Paris, and the New York Marathon, which comes close behind with an average association level of around 14 per cent.

Some non-sporting events, and especially high-profile cultural events, can create high levels of awareness, but none appear to match the Olympics' grip on the public imagination: see Table 5.1.

Both Sydney and Australia, although they are indisputably popular and powerful places, don't appear to have the same range, depth and richness of associations which our panellists ascribe to the more mature place brands such as Italy, London, New York or Paris. These cities and countries have built up their positive global brand equity through countless different channels over several centuries, and arguably have deeper

Table 5.1 Public awareness of major cultural/sporting events

City	Event	Awareness (%)
Rio de Janeiro	Carnival	71.17
Milan	Fashion shows	48.58
Edinburgh	Fringe Festival	27.94
Los Angeles	Academy Awards	27.72
Stockholm	Nobel Awards	27.63
Madrid	Bull Run/Bull Fighting	20.24
San Francisco	Gay Day	19.71
Paris	Fashion shows	18.36

roots. Nation and city brands, for instance Sydney and Australia, can be built on a small number of high-profile and impeccably implemented projects, but the interesting question is how robust they are, and how resilient to negative publicity, if their luck or their good management should turn.

The Summer Olympics is in a category of its own in terms of its ability to "brand" its host city and country, but it's important for countries and cities to understand that simply managing to win the right to host a major sporting or cultural event isn't in itself a way of creating Competitive Identity, or even a lasting international profile. Such events are excellent opportunities for countries to get into the media spotlight for a short period but, as Athens discovered rather too late after hosting the Olympics – probably the biggest PR opportunity that Greece had enjoyed since the sack of Troy – the event itself doesn't automatically do anything for the country's brand. It's a *media opportunity*, not a branding activity in its own right, and the most important thing for countries as they prepare for such events is to know precisely what they are going to say and *prove* about themselves while the show is in town and the global media spotlight is switched on.

The event gives the country permission to make one single, clear, striking point about itself; and if the only point it manages to make is its ability to run an event competently, or that it has money to burn on new facilities and lavish opening ceremonies, then by the time the next host takes over – or even sooner – the world will have forgotten that the event ever took place.

Poetry, ceremony and ritual

Most people naturally assume that the desirable attributes of a Competitive Identity strategy are efficiency, inclusiveness, consensus, vision, expertise, and so forth, but qualities such as poetry, ceremony and ritual, even romance, can also play a significant part in the success of the venture.

This may sound a little whimsical, but there is a practical reason for it. If people are to take their tasks seriously – and few things are more serious for a place than its reputation and the implications this has for its economic, social and cultural development – then it is essential that the importance of those tasks is fully felt by everyone, and fully communicated. The usual methods for communicating importance and gravity in our modern world – portentous phrases in boring documents passed around in dull offices – are ineffective. All they usually produce, not surprisingly, are boring conclusions that nobody objects to and which change precisely nothing.

Far better results can be achieved when we turn instead to the techniques which our (in some ways) wiser forebears employed when it was necessary to make things feel important: ritual, ceremony, poetry, and even a little hocus-pocus. Instead of meeting in committees in meeting rooms, why not create a ritual of meeting in some special, public place; instead of naming the decision-making body in some predictable bureaucratic way, why not give it an imaginative and inspiring title with a potent historical reference; instead of just listening to what economists, pollsters, public affairs specialists and government officials think the future image of the country should be, why not also consult writers, poets, filmmakers, mystics, comedians?

By giving the circumstances and the make-up of the strategic process a little sideways twist, the chances of it developing something genuinely new and genuinely powerful are vastly increased. It's also a good way of making the members of the group understand, and feel, that this isn't "business as usual": they are expected to produce more than procedure. They need to produce extraordinary things, and this is very much harder to achieve when you're in an ordinary mood doing ordinary things in ordinary surroundings.

It's also designed to lighten the mood, even though the issues may be deadly serious. The best solutions to deadly serious problems are nearly always creative, imaginative and daring. They're sometimes even fun. It's designed to make people feel more pride in their city, country or region and in what they're doing. There's little glamour in being on a committee in a committee room, but doing special things with special people in a special place for a special reason feels like an honour and a privilege, and so achieves superior results every time.

When the ultimate "consumer" of a piece of policy is simply other officials, other departments or other governments, then arguably there is no need for that policy to be anything other than efficient and effective. But Competitive Identity is rather different, because its ultimate "consumer" is the general public; the policy has to compete for the public's fleeting and precious attention and interest in a very crowded, very noisy and very exciting public sphere of media, commerce, communication and attention.

For this reason, efficient and effective is only the beginning: it also needs to persuade, to inspire and to motivate. To achieve such lofty aims, "policy as usual" is simply not enough.

CHAPTER 6

Competitive Identity and Development

Not many countries are lucky enough to be economically wealthy, yet virtually all are rich in intangible assets: almost every country on Earth possesses a wide variety of cultural, historical, geographical, human and intellectual capital. But in most cases, for one reason or another, there have not been the right conditions, the ability or the motivation to translate these natural assets into consistent economic performance. However, in a global economy increasingly driven by services, intellectual assets and "virtual" products, the human capital of nations is more than ever the most critical factor in their economic progress, and a lack of conventionally marketable resources is less of a bar to economic development than it has been in the past.

Whether the product being sold is tangible or intangible, intellectual capital plays a vital role in the modern economy by adding value to the product. Without a distinctive and attractive brand, few of today's leading companies could have achieved, still less maintained, their profitability, their market share, or the loyalty of their consumers and employees. And as we have seen, exactly the same principle applies to countries.

Physical products need physical distribution if they are going to generate income. Ideas need branding and marketing. In the knowledge economy, branding is both the strategic discipline and the distribution channel that builds success for smaller countries and turns ideas into wealth.

Much of the economic power on the planet ultimately lies in the hands of the consumer, and brand is the only reliable way to gather that power and plug into it. The economic power of consumers needs to be accumulated before it can be harnessed because it is fragmented: each of us has a small amount of money to spend, but there are billions of us.

Getting us to spend in a concerted way is like herding cats, and can only be achieved by coercion (usually in the form of taxes) or by brands (usually in the form of shopping).

Rich countries understand and create brands and thus plug directly into the economic power of the consumer. Poor and developing countries generally don't do branding, and anyway are separated from the power of the market by middlemen, including importers and distributors and brand owners and especially retailers. The further you are away from the consumer, the less you will benefit from its economic power. So, as I described in *Brand New Justice*, the best way to create wealth in the developing world is to short-circuit that model, and enable poorer countries to build their own brands: to brand their exports, so that they are selling value-added, higher-margin products directly to wealthy consumers in other parts of the world, and to brand themselves for enhanced country of origin effect, and for increased tourism, investment, and so forth.

Taking the brand perspective can do more than give countries a "perceptual edge": it can also provide a route to economic development that in the modern global marketplace may prove more relevant and more productive than the traditional one. The traditional approach is supply based: you see what you can grow on trees or dig up from the ground, use whatever human and industrial resources are available or can be cost-effectively created to process the commodity into a marketable good; and then, almost as an afterthought, you see if you can find a market that's prepared to buy it.

The brand-informed approach to economic development is demand led, and so works in the opposite direction. You start by analysing the brand image of the country, and thus identify what "permission" the marketplace gives the country to produce, and then devise the products and services that would be most enhanced by that country of origin effect.

If, for example, the perception of the marketplace is that the people of a certain country are particularly hardy and the climate of their country very harsh, then hiking gear and energy drinks would be more appropriate branded exports than toys or ceramic tiles; and if there isn't the resource to produce hiking clothes or energy drinks in the country, then you simply have them produced elsewhere, buy them in, and re-sell them with the added value of the country brand attached.

Case notes: A Competitive Identity challenge for Jamaica

Jamaica is undoubtedly a famous country, with an image that is a curious mixture of the very positive and the very negative: some of its holiday resorts are seen as something close to paradise, yet its capital, Kingston, is well-known as one of the more dangerous cities in the world.

It would be difficult for such information not to be generally known when, just to pick one particularly prominent example, the US State Department's Consular Information Sheet on Jamaica features this as its third paragraph, and gets steadily more alarming for about fifteen more paragraphs:

> Gang violence and shootings occur regularly in inner-city areas of Kingston. Some inner-city neighbourhoods are occasionally subject to curfews and police searches. Impromptu demonstrations sometimes occur, during which demonstrators often construct roadblocks or otherwise block the streets.

The facts are certainly well documented, and of course the State Department has a duty of care to warn travellers of the risks involved, so this is not gratuitous "belligerent branding" of the sort I described in Chapter 2; the Jamaican government is doing what it can to solve the problems, but the fact remains that this kind of information is a highly influential component of the way that Jamaica's reputation is built and developed over time.

When the negative perceptions are so strong, there is nothing to be gained and much to be lost by attempting to "spin" the story into something more positive, or to attempt to deny the truth of it. When one is talking about tackling the negative perceptions of violence and criminality, the key is to determine what the appropriate strategy is for resolving the problems themselves, and then to develop a plan for making the solution part of the country's Competitive Identity.

If, for example, the chosen route happened to be a New York-style zero tolerance approach, then organizing an international symposium on urban regeneration in Kingston, with Rudolph Giuliani as keynote speaker, would be a useful experience as well as helping along the CI strategy. And as with every other initiative, one would try to engage all the points of the branding hexagon, so it would need the support of Jamaican brands, ideas from the educational sector, showcased tourism initiatives, case studies on how the music industry can help reverse urban decline, innovative policies from government, and so forth. When all the national stakeholders are working together in a consistent way and in accordance with a common strategy, their combined efforts can be dramatically more effective than when they are working independently.

In reality, the main long-term problem with Jamaica's image is probably not so much the negative elements of crime and violence as the fact that the positive elements in its current image are largely irrelevant to the island's future economy. Jamaica needs to broaden its economic base beyond foreign-owned tourism and the music industry, because this lop-sidedness makes it a vulnerable economy. Tourism is cyclical and seasonal, the cultural and entertainment industry is highly unpredictable, the old industries such as bauxite mining offer no margin and have a high environmental cost, and agriculture is inherently fragile. Jamaica needs to modernize its economy, and it is actively pursuing opportunities in the knowledge economy.

The problem is that Jamaica's current image doesn't give it permission to sell a great many of these knowledge-based products and services. Outsourced call centres, for example, are in some ways an ideal business for Jamaica, but it is an uphill struggle to promote them against the perception that Jamaica is a laid-back holiday destination without significant modern infrastructure and communications. This is particularly unfortunate because one could hardly think of a better place to outsource a call centre than Jamaica due to the likelihood that the people who answer the phone will be happy, friendly, helpful, polite and educated. And here, surely, lies the answer: almost everybody would find those qualities easy to associate with Jamaica, and yet the negative perception – which is an increasingly inaccurate one – of the purely technical issues masks this key asset of the country's reputation which is ultimately of far greater importance for the delivery of this kind of service.

It's as if the image of Jamaica today is a collection of stars in the sky that haven't been joined up: people don't know what the constellation is. So they know there is violence in Kingston, holidays in Negril, riots in Spanish Town, Rasta, Blue Mountain coffee, reggae, jerk chicken and cricket, but there is no constellation; it does not add up to anything more useful than a place to go on holiday. The Competitive Identity task for Jamaica today is to identify its most important future audiences, and to teach them some astrology.

Competitive Identity and the transition economies

Most of the "transition" economies suffer from an image forged during an earlier and very different political era, and which now constantly obstructs their political, economic, cultural and social aspirations.

Slovenia is one example of a state that has succeeded admirably in shaking off the negative perceptions of being "Balkan", and through successful promotion of branded exports (Elan skis, Gorenje appliances, Laško Pivo beer and others), through well-funded tourism campaigns, through NATO and then EU membership. Romania, on the other hand, despite a greatly improved investment climate and notable progress across a wide range of economic, social, cultural and industrial fronts since the time of Ceauşescu, has achieved little in the way of improving its reputation and still finds foreign investment, tourism and exports developing rather slowly. As I mentioned in the previous chapter, a country's reputation stands still at the moment the world heard the last striking thing about it; and because bad or shocking news is generally more intriguing, more durable and more pervasive than good news, there is a strong tendency for national images to accumulate negative equity more easily than the positive kind.

One of the most damaging effects of Communism was the way in which it destroyed the national identity and the nation brands of the countries within the Soviet Union. By stopping the export of their national products and preventing people from travelling abroad, and in many other ways, the Soviet regime effectively deleted the old, distinctive European nation brands – Hungary, Poland, Czechoslovakia, Yugoslavia, Bulgaria, Romania, even Russia itself – that had been created and enriched over centuries of more benign rule. Most of these states are now working hard to rebuild their images and their identities, and it is a slow and painful process.

Spain after General Franco had a similar task to perform, but the recollection of Spain as a lively and democratic Western European nation was more recent – in living memory for many – so the "rebranding" of Spain after 1975 was a relatively straightforward task, akin to the drawing back of a veil. For the countries of Eastern Europe, and especially those without the economic and reputational bonus of EU membership, their brand images must be rebuilt from the rubble, or constructed anew; and in the meantime, the world has changed around them to such an extent that many of their previous reputational assets and equities are no longer competitive, meaningful or relevant to much of their international "audience". Much depends on the land itself and in particular the built environment: places such as Prague, Budapest, Dubrovnik and Ljubljana are fortunate in that their older heritage is still physically evident, and only lacks a narrative to bring it back to life and relevance.

Competitive Identity provides a clue to the way in which newer, smaller and poorer countries can establish and broadcast their true cultural, social and historical identity, and carve out a "perceptual niche" for themselves in the global community.

Joining the global community is connected to brand image, because when supranational bodies such as the European Union, Mercosur, NATO or ASEAN are deciding which countries can join and which can't, there is a clear parallel with brand extension. Accession to bodies such as the European Union is an iceberg: the tip represents the practical, tangible entry requirements; below the waterline are the invisible cultural, historical, social and emotional factors that drive public opinion, as well as the private opinions of decision-makers. Although these decision-makers may not realize it, they are undoubtedly performing a brand strategy exercise when considering members for accession: the European Union, for example, is a powerful and highly respected composite brand – and indeed, for the time being, a remarkably consistent and homogeneous one too – so, just like a large corporation considering the acquisition of a smaller firm, a key question in everybody's mind, whether spoken or not, is to what extent the new brand will enhance (or detract from) the existing one.

I have no doubt that this is part of the reason why there is so much uncertainty about Turkey's accession to the EU: obviously Turkey's image is of a completely different type from the classic EU member state, and nobody really knows whether it will enrich the brand image of Europe – as is my personal belief – or damage it in some irreversible way. Judging by the scores that Turkey receives from the European panellists in the Nation Brands Index, the majority of European citizens are not of my opinion.

A positive image not only makes accession simpler and faster; it also affects to some degree whether the country will benefit from accession. Countries with strong and distinctive reputations stand out from the crowd, retain their national identity and prosper as a result of being a distinctive part of the whole.

Slovenia, for example, had the greatest opportunity it has ever had, or perhaps will have again for centuries, to make its mark on the world when it joined the European Union in May 2004. Suddenly, the spotlight was switched on, and Slovenia stepped onto a stage with 300 million people waiting for it to speak. What would it say? Did it know what it really stood for? Would it, like so many other countries, continue to murmur predictable platitudes about its favourable tax regime, unspoilt beaches, historic towns and skilled workforce, or could it deliver a clear, unique, inspiring, truthful message about itself which people in Europe and beyond would actually take notice of, believe in, remember, and grow to like?

Like several of the accession states, Slovenia had been debating questions of national image and national identity for some time, and had been tinkering with its flag and its slogans; there had even been impassioned arguments about whether the country had the right *name*. It is still widely believed in Slovenia that the flag and the name of the country (which foreigners sometimes confuse with Slovakia) have somehow hindered the country's efforts to promote and position itself in the world, but it is extremely unlikely that these are the real reasons why Slovenia is not yet as famous as many Slovenes would like: that's like blaming the key if your car won't start in the morning. One anonymous place can easily be mistaken for another, but famous countries don't suffer such indignities: Britain and Bhutan sound rather similar, and so do Ireland and Iceland, but people don't get them muddled up half as often as they do with Slovenia and Slovakia, or Niger and Nigeria.

The fact is that Slovenia, like most of the accession states, had no Competitive Identity strategy and no targets for positioning, awareness, recognition or recall, no clear ranking of its overseas markets and audience groups, and no timescale for reaching such targets, so it is impossible for anyone to know whether the confusion with Slovakia is real or anecdotal, or whether it matters, and whether the country's reputation is moving forwards, backwards, or standing still.

The reputation of Slovenia, like that of any other country, needs to be managed, and its government needs to take full responsibility for this crucial national asset, because the country is at a critical moment in its history. Just like a small company after a merger with a larger corporation, the question of whether its unique culture and identity will survive and prosper, or disappear into the larger, greyer, more anonymous composite image of the European Union, is very much a question of brand equity: how well does Slovenia understand its own identity and personality? How competently has it been codified? How good are the Slovenes at communicating it to others, clearly, simply, accurately and powerfully? And how faithfully do they live by it?

An expanding European Union cannot and will not do much to protect and support the fragile cultural identities of all its member states: it is up to them to look after their own interests. And it is the management of their Competitive Identity, as much as any other factor, that will determine which countries will be strengthened by accession, and which will be impoverished by it, and perhaps ultimately annihilated.

Africa and the continent branding effect

Many of the poorest countries in the world have, in effect, no *international* image at all (although of course every place, even the tiniest village, has an image of some sort, even if it only exists in the minds of its nearest neighbours) and thus find themselves considerably disadvantaged in the global economy: they are, in effect, products without packaging in the global supermarket. Such countries generally end up sharing their reputation – often unfairly and inaccurately – with the most prominent and the most infamous countries in their continent.

This effect can be seen quite clearly from the results for the city of Lagos in the City Brands Index (so far, only South Africa is included in the Nation Brands Index, although it is my intention to create an African Nation Brands Index before long). Lagos is the biggest and richest city of Africa's biggest and most populous country, and although no longer the capital of Nigeria is still by any measure the country's first city. It is therefore a good candidate for finding out whether any sub-Saharan city apart from Johannesburg has any brand values that register with our global panel.

The significance of reputation for places such as Lagos and Nigeria is not trivial. If their image is entirely composed of negative elements – such as crime, war, poverty, disease or corruption – then it is unlikely that the city or the country will be able to attract many tourists, foreign investors, trading partners or even consumers for locally produced products.

Lagos ranks at or near the bottom of most of the categories in the City Brands Index, but this is hardly surprising since it is the least well known and least visited of the 30 cities in the Index, and has no world-famous landmarks, personalities, events or achievements. This creates a kind of perceptual vacuum, into which a wide range of generalized African imagery tends to flow. By far the leading association with Lagos is "war", mentioned by 11 per cent of our respondents, an unusually high percentage by any standards: the same percentage, in fact, that associate the United Nations with Geneva. The Biafran War ended in 1970.

When there is little differentiation between the countries in a region, negative equity will always transfer to the entire group (for various reasons, positive equity migrates in a far less equitable way). In exactly the same way, Ecuador, a largely peaceful country which doesn't produce significant quantities of narcotics, is widely believed to be as drug-ridden as Colombia and as lawless as Nicaragua but is almost never credited with the Galápagos Islands, its crown jewel. A relatively prosperous and well-governed African nation such as Botswana ends up sharing perceptions of violence with Rwanda, of corruption with Nigeria, of poverty with Ethiopia and of famine with Sudan; and all live permanently in the shadow of South Africa, because it has begun to develop a distinctive Competitive Identity, and is pulling away from the rest of the continent.

Lagos, like Nigeria itself, and like most cities and most countries in Africa, suffers from this "continent branding effect": none of these places has been able to create a separate, unique international reputation, and so they are obliged to share a generic continent brand called Africa. And Brand Africa, with its simple message of ongoing catastrophe, is promoted with skill, dedication, creativity and vast financial and media resources by aid agencies, international organizations, donor governments and, most prominently, by aid celebrities including Bob Geldof and Bono.

Every time such a celebrity appears before tens of millions of television viewers around the world to make another impassioned plea on behalf of the continent (usually represented by a black logo in the shape of Africa), he is building the brand image of Africa not as 53 countries in various stages of development and struggle for independent existence and identity, but as a uniform, hopeless basket-case. And with each additional promotion of this brand, it becomes harder for countless thousands of places such as Lagos, their companies and entrepreneurs, to break free of these negative associations and start to build a Competitive Identity of their own, or to inspire anything more useful than pity.

This kind of negative branding is the hardest of all to criticize because it is so plainly done with the noblest intentions, and because it does as much good in the short term as it does harm in the long term.

It is no accident that all the successful city brands and nation brands are also rich. Having a powerful and positive international reputation is the cost of entry into the global marketplace, and without it, it is difficult to see how places like Lagos can begin to build their own economies and break their dependence on foreign aid.

For this reason, the primary task of developmental Competitive Identity today is to eliminate "Africa", and replace it with 53 separate, distinctive nations, each with their own story to tell of people, history, culture, products, landscape and government. At the moment, it is Brand Africa that defines the brand images of each country, but it should be the other way round: Africa should be the summation of those individual national reputations. I don't think it's going too far to say that until this issue is widely recognized, and until the governments of each African nation start to take their brand management responsibility seriously, human and economic development in Africa will remain elusive.

During a recent meeting with government officials in Botswana, I was asked how the country could communicate the facts that it is prosperous by African standards, peaceful and beautiful, and has enjoyed a stable democracy for 40 years, when such stories seem simply unable to gain any traction against the overwhelming story of Brand Africa (a story which of course Botswana is obliged to share with every other African nation).

I replied, only half joking, by suggesting that the next time Presidential elections are held in the United States, the Botswana Government might consider sending an election monitoring team to Florida, in order to ensure that the ballot is fair, free and transparent. My suggestion caused a good deal of merriment in Botswana, but it does make one pause and consider the power of Brand Africa that such a suggestion can only be considered a joke, even in the country at whose expense the joke is made. After all, one could argue that America has little more right to send election monitoring teams to Botswana than vice versa. (My subsequent suggestion that the Botswana military might consider sending planes over the Bronx and dropping sacks of grain on the poorer neighbourhoods was received – and, I hasten to add, suggested – with even less seriousness.)

It is one of the most challenging and important roles of Competitive Identity to ensure that the more anonymous states are able to compete on equal terms with the ones that have a distinctive identity and, as far as possible, to level the playing field. In the struggle for competitive advantage in the modern world, the factor of national reputation is becoming more and more significant, and the sooner the development "community" recognizes that perception is as important as reality in the global marketplace, the better its assistance will match the real needs of the countries it aims to help.

Competitiveness beyond capitalism

A crisis of conscience – or perhaps it's fairer to call it a mood of reflection – has gripped the development community. Of course there have always been voices questioning the basic assumptions of economic growth (whether it really confers all the benefits it is intended to; whether it really helps the poor or simply increases the wealth gap; whether it is a suitable model for all countries, irrespective of size, culture, religion, values, aspirations, and so forth); but the reflections seem to be growing more intense by the year.

Today, the difficult questions about development are no longer dismissed as irritating interruptions to the great project of universal economic growth, made by the economically naïve or the politically biased. Joseph Stiglitz's thoughtful review of Benjamin Friedman's *The Moral Consequences of Economic Growth* in *Foreign Affairs*[9] presented us with the fascinating spectacle of world-class economists vying with each other to be perceived as more moral, more culturally sensitive and more versed in "soft" values.

Most interestingly, the question of happiness has begun to emerge in these debates, partly stimulated by H.M. Jigme Singye Wangchuck, the King of Bhutan, and his notion of "Gross National Happiness" as an alternative to GDP. He argues that, whilst his people are indubitably poor and could benefit from increased financial wealth, they are not unhappy, and there is a risk that participating in the global economy will diminish their contentment and perhaps not even improve their material well-being in any predictable, sustainable or even-handed way.

The idea that economic development might not be a panacea – or that, as our parents told us, money might not buy us happiness – is one of the most important to emerge from the development and globalization debate. Consumerism is, without doubt, an incurable disease, and most readers in rich or developing countries will know the ache of wanting and wanting a particular possession, at last buying it, and then feeling the same emptiness gradually return a few days or weeks later. On a recent visit to Bhutan I was struck by the impression that this is a society in the last days of its innocence, where the endless cycle of returning emptiness is still fairly unfamiliar. There are needs, but there appear to be relatively few desires.

Of course, this discussion is highly relevant to the question of Competitive Identity. I have often described the notion of national brand management for economic development as a means of "hacking" one of the first world's most potent and effective tools of wealth creation (after all, brand value, according to some accounts, may represent as much as one-third of all the wealth on the planet) and pressing it into the service of the countries that most need growth. But the wisdom of taking a capitalist tool such as brand management and applying it to developing countries must be closely questioned; and good intentions, whilst they go a long way, are not adequate to ensure that the benefits brought are indeed benefits to all, or that they will prove beneficial in the longer term.

A Buddhist in Bhutan would insist that for this or any process to be a benign one, it must do no harm to any person (whether within the country itself, or as an "externality" in other parts of the world), to any sentient being, to nature, or to future lives. In other words, it is not sufficient to be a good neighbour: one must also be a good ancestor.

Competitive Identity is as much self-defence as proactive behaviour: it is the necessary response (or, in the case of Bhutan, the prudent protection) against the naturally trivializing tendency of international public opinion. As long as public opinion matters – and it matters terribly, because the public is the market – then it is not only legitimate but also vital for countries to do whatever is in their power to ensure that public opinion is as fair, as accurate and as positive as it can be. Countries that don't do this run the risk of being saddled with a reputation that doesn't suit their aims or interests at all, and which is probably based on ignorance, hearsay, confusion or long past events.

I have always held that the market-based view of the world, on which the theory of Competitive Identity is largely predicated, is an inherently peaceful and humanistic model for the relationships between nations. It's based on competition, consumer choice and consumer power; and these concepts are intimately linked to the freedom and power of the individual. For this reason, it seems far more likely to result in lasting world peace than a statecraft based on territory, economic power, ideologies, politics or religion.

In a world dominated by the capitalist system, it is easy to conclude that real competitive advantage can only come from economic, political or military strength, and the unending emphasis on GDP is at the heart of this conception. However, as in any busy marketplace, there is room on the global stage for countries that play by slightly different rules; there is room for niche players, and room for places that compete primarily on cultural excellence or cultural identity, rather than on economic muscle.

Bhutan might, in strictly productive terms, be too small even to be viable as an independent state in the long term, but its real wealth lies in other areas: in its unspoilt landscape, the stability of its social model, its culture and heritage, the wisdom and world-view of its people. Any system that is capable of registering and recognizing such factors as negotiable value – indeed as the components of competitive advantage, is surely worth particular consideration: and since brands are made from values, there is no reason why countries such as Bhutan shouldn't benefit from a reputation that is considerably greater than the size of their economies, land areas or populations would suggest. Economies gain no advantage from being small economies; armies gain no advantage from being small armies; but the small size of a nation such as Bhutan can represent a real brand advantage: to be small, unique, culturally and economically fragile confers a certain precious quality to the national image which big countries can only envy.

Even if the reputation of the country is made of cultural rather than economic factors – even if it's famous for a wealth which is decidedly non-monetary – this still enables it to "punch above its weight" in world affairs, and enjoy an influence which is out of proportion to its GDP. What it chooses to do with that influence is of course its own business, but should economic growth be the ultimate aim then, as every marketer knows, owning a famous brand is the best possible precursor to building a profitable business.

Why else would so many companies, including Google and Skype, find it worthwhile to give away their product or service for free, to gamble profit for profile, and why should the marketplace rate their intangible assets – their brand values and customer relationships – far above any conventional criteria of financial viability? What really counts is having a hold over the imagination of the customer: a unique and appealing proposition that represents a licence to do business with that customer. Countries such as Bhutan have this kind of imaginative power in abundance, and once it has been harnessed, they can use it as leverage to whatever economic, social, political or cultural advances they choose.

One of the great inequalities in the world is the fact that the richer countries have higher profiles than the poorer countries. This is because they have more access to the media, because they tend to export more products and services (which act as particularly powerful ambassadors of national image), because their people travel more freely and thus represent the country more widely, and a whole host of other reasons. Several of them have also enjoyed the cultural and economic "distribution system" of a global empire in the past. This unequal distribution of brand power is well illustrated by the results of the Nation Brands Index, in which all of the nations that are highly ranked are also the wealthiest nations. This fact ensures that the huge discrepancy between their fortunes is robust and durable, because competing is twice as hard with a weak or negative brand image than it is with a strong one.

The success and influence of countries is composed of a balance between what Joseph Nye first termed soft power and hard power. There are times when only coercion can achieve the aims which a government, rightly or wrongly, wishes to pursue, and this is hard power; other ends can only be attained through the exercise of cultural, intellectual or spiritual influence and, as Nye says, "a country may obtain the outcomes it wants in world politics because other countries want to follow it, admiring its values, emulating its example, aspiring to its level of prosperity and openness".[10] Soft power, he says, is making people *want* to do what you want them to do. Competitive Identity is about making people *want* to pay attention to a country's achievements, and believe in its qualities. It is the quintessential modern exemplar of soft power.

For this and for many other reasons, Competitive Identity is an inherently peaceful and humanistic approach to international relations. It's based on competition, consumer choice and consumer power; and these concepts are very intimately linked to the freedom and power of the individual in a democracy. For this reason it's far more likely to result in lasting world peace than a statecraft based on territory, economic power, ideologies, politics or religion.

Competitive Identity, then, whether a nation or city or region is rich or poor, has become an imperative in our modern age of global business, global media and global capital flows. Places that can't or won't develop their own Competitive Identity will find it increasingly difficult to trade and exchange with other nations and win their share of the world's consumers, tourists, capital, investment, talent, cultural exchange, respect and attention.

This is far from being a gloomy picture, however: the conventional system of international power depends on economic, political and military strength, which means that most of the world's countries have lost before the contest begins. At least when the contest is primarily commercial, and the arena more marketplace than battleground, there is room for niche players, small places that can wield an unexpected influence in international affairs because of some distinguishing quality of culture, of history, of intellect, of spirit. Competitive Identity may not be an ideal system in an ideal world, but it is fairer and more humane than the system it is at last beginning to replace.

NOTES

1 According to Interbrand's 2001 survey, 93 per cent of Xerox's market value is attributable to goodwill.

2 See *Traite d'Economie Pure*, Vol. 5, by Maurice Allais (Paris: Imprimerie Nationale, 1952).

3 Quoted by Mark Leonard *et al.* in *Public Diplomacy* (London: Foreign Policy Centre, 2002).

4 See *Brand New Justice – How Branding Places and Products Can Help the Developing World* by Simon Anholt (Oxford: Elsevier, 2003/5).

5 See www.nationbrandsindex.com

6 See www.citybrandsindex.com

7 Abraham H. Maslow, *Eupsychian Management: A Journal* (Homewood, Illinois: R.D. Irwin, 1965).

8 http://www.pikeplacefish.com/aboutus/aboutus_page4.htm

9 www.foreignaffairs.org/20051101fareviewessay84612/joseph-e-stiglitz/the-ethical-economist.html

10 Joseph Nye, *The Paradox of American Power* (Oxford University Press, 2002).